If you are longing for a breath of fresh air in y
for you. Kat Armstrong brings to life both familiar and less familiar Bible stories in such an engaging way that you can't help but see how the God of the past is also working and moving in your present. Through the captivating truths revealed in this series, you will discover more about God's faithfulness, be equipped to move past fear and disappointment, and be empowered to be who you were created to be. If your faith has felt mundane or routine, these words will be a refreshing balm to your soul and a guide to go deeper in your relationship with God.

> **HOSANNA WONG,** international speaker and bestselling author of *How (Not) to Save the World: The Truth about Revealing God's Love to the People Right Next to You*

We are watching a new wave of Bible studies that care about the Bible's big story, from Genesis to Revelation; that plunge Bible readers into the depths of human despair and show them the glories of the Kingdom God plans for creation; and that invite readers to participate in that story in all its dimensions—in the mountains and the valleys. Anyone who ponders these Bible studies will come to terms not only with the storyline of the Bible but also with where each of us fits in God's grand narrative. I heartily commend Kat's **Storyline Bible Studies**.

> **REV. CANON DR. SCOT MCKNIGHT,** professor of New Testament at Northern Seminary

Kat Armstrong is an able trail guide with contagious enthusiasm! In this series, she'll take you hiking through Scripture to experience mountains and valleys, sticks and stones, sinners and saints. If you are relatively new to the Bible or are struggling to see how it all fits together, your trek with Kat will be well worth it. You might even decide that hiking through the Bible is your new hobby.

> **CARMEN JOY IMES,** associate professor of Old Testament at Biola University and author of *Bearing God's Name: Why Sinai Still Matters*

Kat has done two things that I love. She's taken something that is familiar and presented it in a fresh way that is understandable by all, balancing the profound with accessibility. And her trustworthy and constant approach to Bible study equips the participant to emerge from this study with the ability to keep studying and growing more.

MARTY SOLOMON, creator and executive producer of *The BEMA Podcast*

Kat Armstrong takes you into the heart of Scripture so that Scripture can grow in your heart. The **Storyline Bible Studies** have everything: the overarching story of God's redemption, the individual biblical story's historical context, and the text's interpretation that connects with today's realities. Armstrong asks insightful questions that make the Bible come alive and draws authentically on her own faith journey so that readers might deepen their relationship with Jesus. Beautifully written and accessible, the **Storyline Bible Studies** are a wonderful resource for individual or group study.

LYNN H. COHICK, PHD, provost and dean of academic affairs at Northern Seminary

Christians affirm that the Bible is God's Word and provides God's life-giving instruction and encouragement. But what good is such an authoritative and valuable text if God's people don't engage it to find the help the Scriptures provide? Here's where Kat Armstrong's studies shine. In each volume, she presents Bible study as a journey through Scripture that can be transformational. In the process, she enables readers to see the overarching storyline of the Bible and to find their place in that story. In addition, Armstrong reinforces the essential steps that make Bible study life-giving for people seeking to grow in their faith. Whether for individuals, for small groups, or as part of a church curriculum, these studies are ideally suited to draw students into a fresh and invigorating engagement with God's Word.

WILLIAM W. KLEIN, PHD, professor emeritus of New Testament interpretation and author of *Handbook for Personal Bible Study: Enriching Your Experience with God's Word*

You are in for an adventure. In this series, Kat pulls back the curtain to reveal how intentionally God has woven together seemingly disconnected moments in the collective Bible story. Her delivery is both brilliant and approachable. She will invite you to be a curious sleuth as you navigate familiar passages of Scripture, discovering things you'd never seen before. I promise you will never read the living Word the same again.

JENN JETT BARRETT, founder and visionary of The Well Summit

Kat has done it again! The same wisdom, depth, humility, and authenticity that we have come to expect from her previous work is on full display here in her new **Storyline Bible Study** series. Kat is the perfect guide through these important themes and through the story of Scripture: gentle and generous on the one hand, capable and clear on the other. She is a gifted communicator and teacher of God's Word. The format of these studies is helpful too—perfect pacing, just the right amount of new information at each turn, with plenty of space for writing and prayerful reflection as you go and some great resources for further study. I love learning from Kat, and I'm sure you will too. Grab a few friends from your church or neighborhood and dig into these incredible resources together to find your imagination awakened and your faith strengthened.

DAN LOWERY, president of Pillar Seminary

Kat Armstrong possesses something I deeply admire: a sincere and abiding respect for the Bible. Her tenaciousness to know more about her beloved Christ, her commitment to truth telling, and her desire to dig until she mines the deepest gold for her Bible-study readers makes her one of my favorite Bible teachers. I find few that match her scriptural attentiveness and even fewer that embody her humble spirit. This project is stunning, like the rest of her work.

LISA WHITTLE, bestselling author of *Jesus over Everything: Uncomplicating the Daily Struggle to Put Jesus First*, Bible teacher, and podcast host

I'm convinced that the Bible is somehow powerfully simple and beautifully complex. Like a diamond viewed from different angles, Scripture continually confronts my heart in fresh ways. This Bible-study series offers insightful perspectives and gives its participants a refreshing opportunity to admire the character of God and be transformed by the truth of his Word. Our souls need to meander through the minutiae and metanarrative of the Bible, and the **Storyline Bible Studies** help us do both.

KYLE IDLEMAN, senior pastor of Southeast Christian Church and bestselling author of *Not a Fan* and *One at a Time*

VALLEYS

FINDING COURAGE, CONVICTION, AND CONFIDENCE IN LIFE'S LOW POINTS

KAT ARMSTRONG

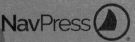

NavPress®

A NavPress resource published in alliance
with Tyndale House Publishers

NavPress is the publishing ministry of The Navigators, an international Christian organization and leader in personal spiritual development. NavPress is committed to helping people grow spiritually and enjoy lives of meaning and hope through personal and group resources that are biblically rooted, culturally relevant, and highly practical.

For more information, visit NavPress.com.

Valleys: Finding Courage, Conviction, and Confidence in Life's Low Points

Copyright © 2023 by Kat Armstrong. All rights reserved.

A NavPress resource published in alliance with Tyndale House Publishers

NavPress and the NavPress logo are registered trademarks of NavPress, The Navigators, Colorado Springs, CO. *Tyndale* is a registered trademark of Tyndale House Ministries. Absence of ® in connection with marks of NavPress or other parties does not indicate an absence of registration of those marks.

The Team:
David Zimmerman, Publisher; Caitlyn Carlson, Acquisitions Editor; Elizabeth Schroll, Copy Editor; Olivia Eldredge, Operations Manager; Julie Chen, Designer; Sarah K. Johnson, Proofreader

Cover illustration by Lindsey Bergsma. Copyright © 2023 by NavPress/The Navigators. All rights reserved.

Author photo by Jody Rodriquez, copyright © 2021. All rights reserved.

Author is represented by Jana Burson of The Christopher Ferebee Agency, christopherferebee.com

Some of the anecdotal illustrations in this book are true to life and are included with the permission of the persons involved. All other illustrations are composites of real situations, and any resemblance to people living or dead is purely coincidental.

For information about special discounts for bulk purchases, please contact Tyndale House Publishers at csresponse@tyndale.com, or call 1-855-277-9400.

ISBN 978-1-64158-584-2

Printed in the United States of America

29	28	27	26	25	24	23
7	6	5	4	3	2	1

For my dad, Ronald K. Obenhaus.
I think you would have loved this.

Contents

A Message from Kat

THE BIBLE IS a literary masterpiece.

Whether you are new to the Christian faith or a seasoned Bible reader, I wrote the **Storyline Bible Studies** to guide you through the storyline of Scripture—each following a person, place, or thing in the Bible. Maybe you are practiced in dissecting a passage or verse and pulling things out of the text to apply to your life. But now you may feel as though your faith is fragmented, coming apart at the seams. The **Storyline Bible Studies** will help you put things back together. You'll discover cohesive, thematic storylines with literary elements and appreciate the Bible as the literary masterpiece that it is.

Tracing a biblical theme, with imagery like mountains and valleys or sticks and stones, will spark your holy curiosity and empower you to cultivate a biblical imagination. I'm praying that your time studying God's Word is an awe-inspiring catalyst to engage and experience God's truth—that you would marvel at the artistry of God's storytelling. And that the Bible will never feel dull or boring ever again.

I wrote *Valleys* when I was starved for encouragement and rebuilding my faith. Do you know that feeling? The valleys of our faith can be miserable places—where our trust in God feels buried. At least that's how it is for me. When I'm in the lowlands, I wonder if all the pain has purpose. And I let my thoughts run wild with fear.

I ask God, *When will this end?*
How will this end?
Why me?
Why, God?

In the middle of that place, do you know what I found? Valleys in the Bible. Valleys whose names I could hardly pronounce. But what took place in these low points felt oh-so-familiar. There in the dark basin of my circumstances I found God, again and again.

And I know you will too.

Together, we are going to study five valleys in the Bible storyline. Some are geographical realities and others are metaphorical places, but God uses them all to teach us about his staying presence. You'll find that each valley represents your lived experience.

Whether you are doubting God's power, finding it harder and harder to face your battles with courage, or feeling like the odds are against you, this Bible study is for you. If you feel like your struggles are undefeatable giants, you're in the right place.

When your faith bottoms out, God is right there with you. He can revive your frail faith. In fact, I'm convinced your lowest points are fertile ground for God to cultivate deep soil—where your trust in his power runs deep.

Deep places for a deeper faith.

Love,

Kat

The Storyline of Scripture

YOUR DECISION TO STUDY THE BIBLE for the next few weeks is no accident—God has brought you here, to this moment. And I don't want to take it for granted. Here, at the beginning, I want to invite you into the most important step you can take, the one that brings the whole of the Bible alive in extraordinary ways: a relationship with Jesus.

The Bible is a collection of divinely inspired manuscripts written over fifteen hundred years by at least forty different authors. Together, the manuscripts make up tens of thousands of verses, sixty-six books, and two testaments. Point being: It's a lot of content.

But the Bible is really just one big story: God's story of redemption. From Genesis to Revelation the Bible includes narratives, songs, poems, wisdom literature, letters, and even apocalyptic prophecies. Yet everything we read in God's Word helps us understand God's love and his plan to be in a relationship with us.

If you hear nothing else, hear this: God loves you.

It's easy to get lost in the vast amount of information in the Bible, so we're going to explore the storyline of Scripture in four parts. And as you locate your experience in the story of the Bible, I hope the story of redemption becomes your own.

PART 1: GOD MADE SOMETHING GOOD.

The big story—God's story of redemption—started in a garden. When God launched his project for humanity, he purposed all of us—his image bearers—to flourish and co-create with him. In the beginning there was peace, beauty, order, and abundant life. The soil was good. Life was good. We rarely hear this part of our story, but it doesn't make it less true. God created something good—and that includes you.

PART 2: WE MESSED IT UP.

If you've ever thought, *This isn't how it's supposed to be*, you're right. It's not. We messed up God's good world. Do you ever feel like you've won gold medals in messing things up? Me too. All humanity shares in that brokenness. We are imperfect. The people we love are imperfect. Our systems are jacked, and our world is broken. And that's on us. We made the mess, and we literally can't help ourselves. We need to be rescued from our circumstances, the systems in which we live, and ourselves.

PART 3: JESUS MAKES IT RIGHT.

The good news is that God can clean up all our messes, and he does so through the life, death, and resurrection of Jesus Christ. No one denies that Jesus lived and died. That's just history. It's the empty tomb and the hundreds of eyewitnesses who saw Jesus after his death that make us scratch our heads. Because science can only prove something that is repeatable, we are dependent upon the eyewitness testimonies of Jesus' resurrection for this once-in-history moment. If Jesus rose from the dead—and I believe he did—Jesus is exactly who he said he was, and he accomplished exactly what had been predicted for thousands of years. He restored us. Jesus made *it*, all of it, right. He can forgive your sins and connect you to the holy God through his life, death, and resurrection.

PART 4: ONE DAY, GOD WILL MAKE ALL THINGS NEW.

The best news is that this is not as good as it gets. A day is coming when Christ will return. He's coming back to re-create our world: a place with no tears, no pain, no suffering, no brokenness, no helplessness—just love. God will make all things new. In the meantime, God invites you to step into his storyline, to join him in his work of restoring all things. Rescued restorers live with purpose and on mission: not a life devoid of hardship, but one filled with enduring hope.

RESPONDING TO GOD'S STORYLINE

If the storyline of Scripture feels like a lightbulb turning on in your soul, that, my friend, is the one true, living God, who eternally exists as Father, Son, and Holy Spirit. God is inviting you into a relationship with him to have your sins forgiven and secure a place in his presence forever. When you locate your story within God's story of redemption, you begin a lifelong relationship with God that brings meaning, hope, and restoration to your life.

Take a moment now to begin a relationship with Christ:

God, I believe the story of the Bible, that Jesus is Lord and you raised him from the dead to forgive my sins and make our relationship possible. Your storyline is now my story. I want to learn how to love you and share your love with others. Amen.

If you confess with your lips that Jesus is Lord and believe in your heart that God raised him from the dead, you will be saved.

ROMANS 10:9, NRSV

How to Use This Bible Study

THE **STORYLINE BIBLE STUDIES** are versatile and can be used for

- ▼ individual study (self-paced),
- ▼ small groups (five- or ten-lesson curriculum), or
- ▼ church ministry (semester-long curriculum).

INDIVIDUAL STUDY

Each lesson in the *Valleys* Bible study is divided into four fifteen- to twenty-minute parts (sixty to eighty minutes of individual study time per lesson). You can work through the material one part at a time over a few different days or all in one sitting. Either way, this study will be like anything good in your life: What you put in, you get out. Each of the four parts of each lesson will help you practice Bible-study methods.

SMALL GROUPS

Working through the *Valleys* Bible study with a group could be a catalyst for life change. Although the Holy Spirit can teach you truth when you read the Bible on your own, I want to encourage you to gather a small group together to work through this study for these reasons:

- God himself is in communion as one essence and three persons: Father, Son, and Holy Spirit.
- Interconnected, interdependent relationships are hallmarks of the Christian faith life.
- When we collaborate with each other in Bible study, we have access to the viewpoints of our brothers and sisters in Christ, which enrich our understanding of the truth.

For this Bible study, every small-group member will need a copy of the *Valleys* study guide. In addition, I've created a free downloadable small-group guide that includes

- discussion questions for each lesson,
- Scripture readings, and
- prayer prompts.

Whether you've been a discussion leader for decades or just volunteered to lead a group for the first time, you'll find the resources you need to create a loving atmosphere for men and women to grow in Christlikeness. You can download the small-group guide using this QR code.

CHURCH MINISTRY

Church and ministry leaders: Your work is sacred. I know that planning and leading through a semester of ministry can be both challenging and rewarding. That's why every **Storyline Bible Study** is written so that you can build modular semesters of ministry. The *Valleys* Bible study is designed to complement the *Mountains*

Bible study. Together, *Mountains* and *Valleys* can support a whole semester of ministry seamlessly, inviting the people you lead into God's Word and making your life simpler.

To further equip church and ministry leaders, I've created *The Leader's Guide*, a free digital resource. You can download *The Leader's Guide* using this QR code.

The Leader's Guide offers these resources:

- ▼ a sample ministry calendar for a ten-plus-lesson semester of ministry,
- ▼ small-group discussion questions for each lesson,
- ▼ Scripture readings for each lesson,
- ▼ prayer prompts for each lesson,
- ▼ five teaching topics for messages that could be taught in large-group settings, and
- ▼ resources for deeper study.

SPECIAL FEATURES

However you decide to utilize the *Valleys* Bible study, whether for individual, self-paced devotional time; as a small-group curriculum; or for semester-long church ministry, you'll notice several stand-out features unique to the **Storyline Bible Studies**:

- ▼ gospel presentation at the beginning of each Bible study;
- ▼ full Scripture passages included in the study so that you can mark up the text and keep your notes in one place;
- ▼ insights from diverse scholars, authors, and Bible teachers;
- ▼ an emphasis on close readings of large portions of Scripture;
- ▼ following one theme instead of focusing on one verse or passage;
- ▼ Christological narrative theology without a lot of church-y words; and
- ▼ retrospective or imaginative readings of the Bible to help Christians follow the storyline of Scripture.

You may have studied the Bible by book, topic, or passage before; all those approaches are enriching ways to read the Word of God. The **Storyline Bible Studies** follow a literary thread to deepen your appreciation for God's master plan of redemption and develop your skill in connecting the Old Testament to the New.

THE VALLEYS STORYLINE

WHEN WAS THE LAST TIME you found yourself in a low place? That's where I was as I started to trace God's work in the valleys of Scripture. In fact, as I told my closest group of friends, I was at one of my lowest points in ministry. In the middle of a global pandemic, I'd pivoted till I was dizzy. God had showed up in mighty ways . . . but I was exhausted and ready to give up hope.

As I walked through my personal valley, I was surprised to discover that the valleys in the Bible have far more meaning than just as geographical markers or pins on an ancient map. In his literary genius, God repurposes valley settings throughout Scripture to signal tests of faith—and the deepening of confidence in the One who is with us in the valley.

I'm still struggling through my same valley in many ways. But I'll tell you this: The comfort and encouragement I received from my journey through the Bible's valleys has changed me to my core. My circumstances may have not yet changed for the better, but my friends would tell you that *I've* changed. Something has shifted. God did that as I studied the valleys storyline in Scripture.

In *Valleys*, we're going to explore

- ▼ *Numbers 13–14*: the Valley of Eshkol, where Moses' spies scouted the Promised Land;
- ▼ *Judges 4–5*: the Valley of Kishon, where Deborah and Jael defeated their enemy;
- ▼ *1 Samuel 17*: the Valley of Elah, where David fought Goliath;
- ▼ *Psalm 23*: the Valley of Death, where God comforts scared people; and
- ▼ *Ezekiel 37*: the Valley of Dry Bones, where Ezekiel prophesied Israel's restoration.

We're going to do this by looking at each valley through four different lenses:

- ▼ **PART 1: CONTEXT.** Do you ever feel dropped into a Bible story disoriented? Part 1 will introduce you to the valley you're going to study and its scriptural context. Getting your bearings before you read will enable you to answer the question *What am I about to read?*

- ▼ **PART 2: SEEING.** Do you ever read on autopilot? I do too. Sometimes I finish reading without a clue as to what just happened. A better way to read the Bible is to practice thoughtful, close reading of Scripture to absorb the message God is offering to us. That's why part 2 includes close Scripture reading and observation questions to empower you to answer the question *What is the story saying?*

- ▼ **PART 3: UNDERSTANDING.** If you've ever scratched your head after reading your Bible, part 3 will give you the tools to understand the author's intended meaning both for the original audience and for you. Plus you'll practice connecting the Old and New Testaments to get a fuller picture of God's unchanging grace. Part 3 will enable you to answer the question *What does it mean?*

▼ **PART 4: RESPONDING.** The purpose of Bible study is to help you become more Christlike; that's why part 4 will include journal space for your reflection on and responses to the content and a blank checklist for actionable next steps. You'll be able to process what you're learning so that you can live out the concepts and pursue Christlikeness. Part 4 will enable you to answer the questions *What truths is this passage teaching?* and *How do I apply this to my life?*

One of my prayers for you, as a curious Bible reader, is that our journey through this study will help you cultivate a biblical imagination so that you're able to make connections throughout the whole storyline of the Bible. In each lesson, I'll do my best to include a few verses from different places in the Bible that are connected to our valley stories. In the course of this study, we'll see the way God shows up in valleys throughout his Word—and get a glimpse of how he might show up in our lives today.

God's Word is so wonderful, I hardly know how to contain my excitement. Feel free to geek out with me; let your geek flag fly high, my friends. When we can see how interrelated all the parts of Scripture are to each other, we'll find our affection for God stirred as we see his artistic brilliance unfold.

TRUSTING GOD WITH YOUR GIANT-SIZED DOUBTS

**VALLEY OF ESHKOL:
WHERE MOSES' SPIES SCOUT THE PROMISED LAND**

SCRIPTURE: NUMBERS 13–14

PART 1

CONTEXT

Before you begin your study, we will start with the context of the story we are about to read together: the setting, both cultural and historical; the people involved; and where our passage fits in the larger setting of Scripture. All these things help us make sense of what we're reading. Understanding the context of a Bible story is fundamental to reading Scripture well. Getting your bearings before you read will enable you to answer the question *What am I about to read?*

TELL ME IF THIS SOUNDS FAMILIAR.

You feel like your world cracked. The bottom fell out of your plans or relationships or health. You're at your lowest of lows. You not only have "friends in low places,"[1] you've got caverns in your soul.

Maybe you've been there before. Maybe you're there right now. The human condition is such that we'll all likely be there again.

The dips in life might cause us to question God. That's normal. Everyone who follows Jesus will experience a crisis of faith at some point in their journey. When your doubts seem to erode your faith, it's hard to trust God's plans and his goodness. But God can handle your doubts and your questions.

In this lesson, we are going to read from the book of Numbers about a small group of spies sent by Moses to scout the Promised Land. The twelve spies, including a man named Caleb, find that the Valley of Eshkol is just as fertile as

God promised. But there is a big problem: Giants occupy the land. For most of the spies, fear leads the way. Doubts set in. And the Israelites end up experiencing decades of consequences because they can't bring themselves to look past the giants.

But Caleb is different.

My husband, Aaron, wanted to name our one and only child Caleb, after this man in the Valley of Eshkol story who kept his eyes on God. This valley story means a lot to me and my family. Embedded in my son's name is an aspirational blessing and a legacy of faith. Maybe soon, Caleb Armstrong will reach for his Bible and turn to the pages in Numbers 13 and 14 to remind himself who else has lived with his name. My prayer is that his connection to this man will help him trust God with his own giant-sized doubts.

Valley of Eshkol: You might see this referred to as the Valley of Eshcol elsewhere, depending on which translation you reference. I followed the spelling of the translation I quoted for this passage.

If you don't spend a lot of time reading the book of Numbers, you're in good company. I rarely do either.

Every time I revisit a story in Numbers, I reorient myself to God's storyline of redemption to find my bearings. The story of the Valley of Eshkol in Numbers 13 and 14 connects to everything that has happened before it and everything that will come after.

On page 1 of the Bible, God creates the first man and woman in his image and starts a relationship with his people. Very soon after, God launches his project—to see his family flourish. But Adam and Eve rebel against God's good plan to bless the whole world. This is the first time in the Bible, of many, that God forgives sin and creates a way for people to remain in relationship with him.

In one of God's many acts of grace, he chooses Abraham and his family to bless the world because Adam and Eve failed to. Most of the book of Genesis is about Abraham's family line. (And let's just say that if Abraham had his own Netflix series, he would have won an Emmy.)

By the time we get to the next book of the Bible, Exodus, we find God's people enslaved under the Egyptians. God acts again, rescuing his people through a man named Moses, who leads the Israelites out of oppression, through the Red

Sea, and to Mount Sinai in the wilderness. Again God proves that he longs to forgive—and restore a loving relationship with—his people. At Mount Sinai, he does this through a covenant that reassures the Israelites of their inheritance: the Promised Land. This would be a place of fruitfulness and abundance, overflowing with plenty, a home for God's people to settle and grow.

Right off the bat, you and I should sense that the Promised Land is a sacred echo of the Garden of Eden, a place of promise and hope. The Promised Land, like Eden before it, points us to our bright future with God and helps us tangibly understand his uncompromising, unending love.

In the Valley of Eshkol, we see that Caleb takes God at his word, trusting in the promise even in the face of doubt—while those around him give way to fear. Like me, you may find a deep connection with the people who are struggling with fear, but my hope for us all is that we will emulate Caleb's faith. As we study this low point in the Israelites' journey, I want us to see that our God is powerful enough to overcome the giants in our lives.

If you are in the valley of doubt, I have good news for you: *God can be trusted.*

1. **PERSONAL CONTEXT: What is going on in your life right now that might impact how you understand this Bible story?**

2. **SPIRITUAL CONTEXT: If you've never studied this Bible story before, what piques your curiosity? If you've studied this passage before, what impressions and insights do you recall? What problems or concerns might you have with the passage?**

PART 2

SEEING

Seeing the text is vital if we want the heart of the Scripture passage to sink in. We read slowly and intentionally through the text with the context in mind. As we practice close, thoughtful reading of Scripture, we pick up on phrases, implications, and meanings we might otherwise have missed. Part 2 includes close Scripture reading and observation questions to empower you to answer the question *What is the story saying?*

1. **Read Numbers 13:1–25 and circle every name of a person or place.**

13 The LORD said to Moses, [2] "Send some men to explore the land of Canaan, which I am giving to the Israelites. From each ancestral tribe send one of its leaders."

[3] So at the LORD's command Moses sent them out from the Desert of Paran. All of them were leaders of the Israelites. [4] These are their names:

from the tribe of Reuben, Shammua son of Zakkur;

[5] from the tribe of Simeon, Shaphat son of Hori;

[6] from the tribe of Judah, Caleb son of Jephunneh;

[7] from the tribe of Issachar, Igal son of Joseph;

[8] from the tribe of Ephraim, Hoshea son of Nun;

⁹ from the tribe of Benjamin, Palti son of Raphu;

¹⁰ from the tribe of Zebulun, Gaddiel son of Sodi;

¹¹ from the tribe of Manasseh (a tribe of Joseph), Gaddi son of Susi;

¹² from the tribe of Dan, Ammiel son of Gemalli;

¹³ from the tribe of Asher, Sethur son of Michael;

¹⁴ from the tribe of Naphtali, Nahbi son of Vophsi;

¹⁵ from the tribe of Gad, Geuel son of Maki.

¹⁶ These are the names of the men Moses sent to explore the land. (Moses gave Hoshea son of Nun the name Joshua.)

¹⁷ When Moses sent them to explore Canaan, he said, "Go up through the Negev and on into the hill country. ¹⁸ See what the land is like and whether the people who live there are strong or weak, few or many. ¹⁹ What kind of land do they live in? Is it good or bad? What kind of towns do they live in? Are they unwalled or fortified? ²⁰ How is the soil? Is it fertile or poor? Are there trees in it or not? Do your best to bring back some of the fruit of the land." (It was the season for the first ripe grapes.)

²¹ So they went up and explored the land from the Desert of Zin as far as Rehob, toward Lebo Hamath. ²² They went up through the Negev and came to Hebron, where Ahiman, Sheshai and Talmai, the descendants of Anak, lived. (Hebron had been built seven years before Zoan in Egypt.) ²³ When they reached the Valley of Eshkol, they cut off a branch bearing a single cluster of grapes. Two of them carried it on a pole between them, along with some pomegranates and figs. ²⁴ That place was called the Valley of Eshkol because of the cluster of grapes the Israelites cut off there. ²⁵ At the end of forty days they returned from exploring the land.

NUMBERS 13:1-25

2. **Using Numbers 13:17-20, fill out this imaginary scout report as if you were Caleb the spy.**

SPY NAME: _____

Date: after Sinai

Mission: scout the Promised Land

Location: Valley of _____

Are the people in this valley strong or weak?

□ strong

□ weak

Are the people in this valley few or many?

□ few

□ many

Is the Promised Land good or bad?

□ good

□ bad

Are the towns fortified or unwalled?

□ fortified

□ unwalled

Just as Caleb's name means a lot to our family, the name Eshkol has significance. Eshkol means "cluster," as in a cluster of grapes.[2] Eshkol has symbolic meaning as an area with deep soil where lush produce can grow. I can barely pronounce the word with confidence, but I have no doubt God intended us to find his valley imagery dripping with hope.

3. Based on Numbers 13:23-24, what did the spies choose to bring back to camp as evidence of the Promised Land's fertility? Check all that apply.

☐ figs
☐ milk
☐ honey
☐ grapes
☐ pomegranates

When Aaron and I traveled to Sydney, Australia, we toured several vineyards. We cupped ripe grape clusters—still hanging from their vine—and drank in their sweet smell before a little wine tasting. We made memories to last a lifetime, marveling at the rows and rows of firmly planted vines and savoring the taste of God's creation.

Maybe one of the points God is making in the scouts' preview of the Promised Land is that his word is as good as the grapes. If he promised to fill the land with fruit, and he *did* fill it with fruit, maybe the blessing he promised this people—to occupy land they did not yet own—was a sure thing.

Like the Israelites, I struggle to trust God, even though evidence of his faithfulness is all around me. Often, I choose to disregard the truth of God's character and the sureness of his promises to focus on all the reasons things won't work out.

4. According to Numbers 13:25, how long did the spies scout the Promised Land?

a. forty days
b. seven days
c. we don't know for sure

The forty days the twelve spies spent scouting the land is a sacred echo of Noah's forty days of rainfall while he was in the ark during the Flood. The Valley of Eshkol signals back to the first book of the Bible *and* propels us forward in the story of redemption—to Christ's forty days of testing in the wilderness. Noah, Caleb, and Jesus all know a thing or two about forty harrowing days of adventure.

In the Bible, a forty-day window is a pattern: enough time to test our faith. And that's what we see happening to Caleb in the Valley of Eshkol.

5. **Read Numbers 13:26–14:10. Every time someone speaks, draw an emoji in the margin that summarizes their statement.**

26 They came back to Moses and Aaron and the whole Israelite community at Kadesh in the Desert of Paran. There they reported to them and to the whole assembly and showed them the fruit of the land. 27 They gave Moses this account: "We went into the land to which you sent us, and it does flow with milk and honey! Here is its fruit. 28 But the people who live there are powerful, and the cities are fortified and very large. We even saw descendants of Anak there. 29 The Amalekites live in the Negev; the Hittites, Jebusites and Amorites live in the hill country; and the Canaanites live near the sea and along the Jordan."

30 Then Caleb silenced the people before Moses and said, "We should go up and take possession of the land, for we can certainly do it."

31 But the men who had gone up with him said, "We can't attack those people; they are stronger than we are." 32 And they spread among the Israelites a bad report about the land they had explored. They said, "The land we explored devours those living in it. All the people we saw there are of great size. 33 We saw the Nephilim there (the descendants of Anak come from the Nephilim). We seemed like grasshoppers in our own eyes, and we looked the same to them."

14 That night all the members of the community raised their voices and wept aloud. 2 All the Israelites grumbled against Moses and Aaron, and the whole assembly said to them, "If only we had died in Egypt! Or in

this wilderness! ³ Why is the LORD bringing us to this land only to let us fall by the sword? Our wives and children will be taken as plunder. Wouldn't it be better for us to go back to Egypt?" ⁴ And they said to each other, "We should choose a leader and go back to Egypt."

⁵ Then Moses and Aaron fell facedown in front of the whole Israelite assembly gathered there. ⁶ Joshua son of Nun and Caleb son of Jephunneh, who were among those who had explored the land, tore their clothes ⁷ and said to the entire Israelite assembly, "The land we passed through and explored is exceedingly good. ⁸ If the LORD is pleased with us, he will lead us into that land, a land flowing with milk and honey, and will give it to us. ⁹ Only do not rebel against the LORD. And do not be afraid of the people of the land, because we will devour them. Their protection is gone, but the LORD is with us. Do not be afraid of them."

¹⁰ But the whole assembly talked about stoning them. Then the glory of the LORD appeared at the tent of meeting to all the Israelites.

NUMBERS 13:26–14:10

6. **After reviewing Numbers 13:26-33, list the pros and cons of the Promised Land.**

Pros	Cons

I love a pro/con list when I am making a hard decision. But when it comes to trusting God, lists are not useful—because God's power outweighs any measure on a scale.

7. Based on Numbers 14:1-5, how would you describe the Israelites' reaction to the twelve spies' report about the Promised Land?

The people's reaction reminds me of one of Caleb (Armstrong)'s epic toddler meltdowns . . . over a vacuum. Yes, you read that right. The little dude was obsessed with the sound and use of a vacuum. (Future wife of Caleb: You're welcome.) As soon as we asked Caleb to release his grip on his baby vacuum, he unleashed big crocodile tears. Just as his reaction revealed immaturity, the reaction of the people to their leaders in our valley story shows just how far they had to go in trusting God. And if I'm honest, their response is often my own when I am afraid.

8. Using Numbers 14:6-9, write a paraphrase of Caleb's speech.

9. After Caleb's compelling speech to trust God's power over the giants in the Valley of Eshkol, what did the people threaten to do to their leaders? (See Numbers 14:10.)

The people's threats against Caleb, Joshua, Moses, and Aaron give new meaning to the common phrase *scared to death*. See a people afraid for their lives, and you'll find an angry mob turning on their leaders. Our doubt may come from reasonable fears, but how will we respond to that doubt?

PART 3

UNDERSTANDING

Now that we've finished a close reading of the Scriptures, we're going to spend some time on interpretation: doing our best to understand what God was saying to the original audience and what he's teaching us through the process. But to do so, we need to learn his ways and consider how God's Word would have been understood by the original audience before applying the same truths to our own lives. "Scripture interpretation" may sound a little stuffy, but understanding what God means to communicate to us in the Bible is crucial to enjoying a close relationship with Jesus. Part 3 will enable you to answer the question *What does it mean?*

THE VALLEY OF ESHKOL is far more than simply the location for Moses' spy mission. This low place in Scripture points us toward God's power to deliver on his promises—even when we are in a valley of doubt.

Caleb displayed courage when he trusted God's power over the giants of the Valley of Eshkol. For Caleb, occupying the Promised Land was as sure as God is strong. But for the rest of the Israelites, the scouts' report was a failed faith test.

Notice with me the spiral that happens as the people's doubts take over. First, God promises that he will give the Israelites the Promised Land, telling them to scout it out so they can see just how good his blessings will be. But instead of focusing on the goodness of the land and the greatness of its giver, the Israelites fixate on legitimate fears about the fortified cities occupied by giants. Naturally, they start comparing themselves to the giants and assume that their average-sized selves are too small. Feeling defeated, the Israelites start to blame their leaders for leading them astray, and worst of all, they doubt God's capabilities. Their rebellion delays God's blessing—*by forty years*. Forty years of wandering in the desert, y'all. What took forty days to test became forty years of testing.

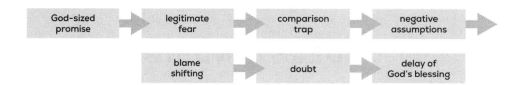

Listen, this whole situation feels like someone ripped a page out of my fear-inducing playbook. I've gone through this progression time and time again in my own life. And something I've learned is that every step unearths a deeper question. Every piece of fear is a choice. How will I answer?

The people certainly failed in many aspects, but the writer points specifically to, and takes great care to draw out, their failure to believe God. Thus this passage intends to show that the people failed to inherit the Promised Land and hence died in the wilderness without inheriting the blessing, not so much for a specific act of disobedience or for fear of the battles that lay ahead, but rather for the simple fact of their unbelief. They failed to trust God.[3]

John H. Sailhamer,
The Pentateuch as Narrative

Doubt isn't a sin. Fears can be legitimate. But what we choose out of our doubt and fear either moves us closer to God or further away.

1. **What would the Valley of Eshkol story have meant to the Israelites at the time?**

2. **What would the Valley of Eshkol story have meant to Israelites in later generations?**

MAKING CONNECTIONS

An important part of understanding the meaning of a Bible passage is getting a sense of its place in the broader storyline of Scripture. When we make connections between different parts of the Bible, we get a glimpse of the unity and cohesion of the Scriptures.

If you know a thing or two, or a hundred, about struggling with unbelief, stick with me. As we connect the testing in the Valley of Eshkol to instructions in the New Testament and our ultimate hope in God, we'll find encouragement for our journey.

The apostle Paul was a first-century church planter and missionary who contributed several letters to the New Testament. In one of his letters, he addresses the stress of Christians living in a place called Corinth. Paul's admonition is as intense as I imagine him to be in real life. And the allusions he uses to make his point are all connected to the Israelites' time wandering in the desert—their forty years of testing after their failure at the Valley of Eshkol. According to Paul, examining their missteps can guide us through our own valleys of doubt.

3. **Read 1 Corinthians 10:1-13 and underline everything Paul has to say about temptation in this passage.**

10 Now I do not want you to be unaware, brothers and sisters, that our ancestors were all under the cloud, all passed through the sea, ² and all were baptized into Moses in the cloud and in the sea. ³ They all ate the same spiritual food, ⁴ and all drank the same spiritual drink. For they drank from the spiritual rock that followed them, and that rock was Christ. ⁵ Nevertheless God was not pleased with most of them, since they were struck down in the wilderness.

⁶ Now these things took place as examples for us, so that we will not desire evil things as they did. ⁷ Don't become idolaters as some of them were; as it is written, The people sat down to eat and drink, and got up to party. ⁸ Let us not commit sexual immorality as some of them did, and in a single day twenty-three thousand people died. ⁹ Let us not test Christ as some of them did and were destroyed by snakes. ¹⁰ And don't grumble as some of them did, and were killed by the destroyer. ¹¹ These things happened to them as examples, and they were written for our instruction, on whom the ends of the ages have come. ¹² So, whoever thinks he stands must be careful not to fall. ¹³ No temptation has come upon you except what is common to humanity. But God is faithful; he

will not allow you to be tempted beyond what you are able, but with the temptation he will also provide the way out so that you may be able to bear it.

1 CORINTHIANS 10:1-13, CSB

4. In 1 Corinthians 10:13, what three reasons does Paul give for hope when our faith is being tested?

1.

2.

3.

Several New Testament authors allude to the Valley of Eshkol story. One passage that has become a favorite of mine is from the book of Hebrews. We can't know who the author is for sure, but this person knew the Scriptures well: They connected our faith in Christ to God's people in the Old Testament.

5. Read Hebrews 3:12-19 and underline what the author of Hebrews suggests doing to remain faithful to God when we have a hard time believing him.

[12] See to it, brothers and sisters, that none of you has a sinful, unbelieving heart that turns away from the living God. [13] But encourage one another daily, as long as it is called "Today," so that none of you may be hardened by sin's deceitfulness. [14] We have come to share in Christ, if indeed we hold our original conviction firmly to the very end. [15] As has just been said:

> "Today, if you hear his voice,
>   do not harden your hearts
>   as you did in the rebellion."

[16] Who were they who heard and rebelled? Were they not all those Moses led out of Egypt? [17] And with whom was he angry for forty years? Was

it not with those who sinned, whose bodies perished in the wilderness? [18] And to whom did God swear that they would never enter his rest if not to those who disobeyed? [19] So we see that they were not able to enter, because of their unbelief.

HEBREWS 3:12-19

God offers us a way forward through this valley, and it doesn't involve dismissing or ignoring our doubts. Instead, as the author of Hebrews shows us, we hold firm to "the reality that we had at the start" (Hebrews 3:14, csb)—the promise God has given us from the beginning. Even in the Valley of Eshkol, even in our doubt, he reminds us what he created us for and has, in Christ, made us participants in: unbroken relationship with God and eternal provision in his presence. That promise echoes from the Garden of Eden through the Valley of Eshkol all the way toward the Garden City, Zion, in Revelation 21 and 22.

GARDENS IN THE BIBLE

Place	Purpose	Provision
the Garden of Eden	a parcel of promise to enjoy a relationship with God, our Creator	The trees in the Garden produced fruit for Adam and Eve to eat.
the Valley of Eshkol	a part of the Promised Land that God ensured the Israelites would enjoy as a benefit of their relationship with him	The clusters of fruit Moses' spies sampled in the Valley of Eshkol are a sacred echo of the Tree of Life in the Garden of Eden.
the Garden City, Zion	the central location for God's presence in the new heaven and new earth	God will host a banquet in the Garden City, Zion, providing all the fruit we'll need to live forever in his presence.

If you're having a hard time counting on God, you're not alone—it's part of the human experience. But on the other side of doubt is a deeper relationship with God and the abundant life he offers. Giants may be in the land, but you have not been abandoned. God is with you and for you, and he will carry you into the promise.

▼ ▼ ▼

Let's take a look at our storyline.

THE VALLEYS STORYLINE OF SCRIPTURE

Location	Scripture	Protagonist
Valley of Eshkol	Numbers 13–14	Caleb
Valley of Kishon	Judges 4–5	Deborah
Valley of Elah	1 Samuel 17	David
Valley of Death	Psalm 23	the psalmist
Valley of Dry Bones	Ezekiel 37	Israel

Antagonist	Giants	Meaning
Canaanites	giants (the Anakim) living in the Promised Land	a valley where you can choose to trust
Canaanites	a giant-sized army: nine hundred iron chariots among King Jabin's forces	a valley where you can choose to face your battles with courage and conviction
Philistines	Goliath, a Philistine giant	a valley where you can choose to stay brave when the odds are against you
unsafe people and the depths of hardship	the giants of threat and danger	a valley where you can choose to follow the Good Shepherd through many dangers
Babylonian exile	the giants of hopelessness and death	a valley where you can choose to let God resurrect your hope

1. What valley are you walking through? How does this lesson remind you of God's presence in your valley?

2. What did you learn about God's character in this lesson?

3. How should these truths shape your faith community and change you?

RESPONDING

The purpose of Bible study is to help you become more Christlike; that's why part 4 will include journaling space for your reflection on and responses to the content and a blank checklist for actionable next steps. You'll be able to process what you're learning so that you can live out the concepts and pursue Christlikeness. Part 4 will enable you to answer the questions *What truths is this passage teaching?* and *How do I apply this to my life?*

FOR MY SON'S FIRST BIRTHDAY, I had an art print designed and framed for his room. It created a striking contrast with the babyish décor. The piece has a few simple words at the top and a painted valley at the bottom that represents the Valley of Eshkol. If you didn't know the backstory, the valley looks like an empty flatland. But there is green at the bottom, pointing to life—doubt reframed into trust.

My hope is that Caleb will keep the art as he grows and feel proud of it when he's settled into his own home. (I know, it's a long shot, but a mother can dream.) It says this:

No giants are too big.
We are not grasshoppers.
You won't die in the desert.
Slavery is not better.

God promised us.
Go get the land.

Not exactly a Mother Goose nursery rhyme, is it? But if Caleb Armstrong remembers anything about his room, I hope it is those words. I'm praying that the tangible picture hanging on his wall will serve as a reminder that God has promised to overpower his giants. Giants of evil, of fear, and of circumstance.

I think one of the messages you and I are supposed to take away from the Valley of Eshkol story is about reframing. We can feel low because we have so many doubts and also be deep in trust. You see, when our valley of doubt feels like death, it may in fact be a cradle—the birthplace for a deeper faith.

When you find yourself laid low, kneel and remember that the soil is deep in these valleys—and deep soil makes for the best farmland. As you cultivate a life of faith, dig deep when you are in a valley. It's an opportunity to trust God with your giant-sized doubts.

1. NO GIANTS ARE TOO BIG.

Your giants are big, I know. Whether it's a bad breakup or a painful divorce, the ache of infertility or the loss of a loved one, the wounds of betrayal or the fog of confusion—whatever you are facing, the pain and fear are real. These oversized problems threaten to overpower you. But they cannot overpower God. No giants are too big for your God.

2. WE ARE NOT GRASSHOPPERS.

When you are surrounded by giants, getting squashed is a legitimate fear. But you are not a grasshopper. You are a Christ follower filled with the power of the Holy Spirit. When your instinct is to cower in fear, trust in God's immeasurable strength. He towers over our problems and makes our enemy run away scared.

3. SLAVERY IS NOT BETTER.

Your season in the valley of doubt will tempt you to turn away from your faith in God and back to whatever brings you temporary comfort. But your relationship with God has shown you, perhaps over and over, that what you left behind was no good for you. It didn't serve you—you served it, like a slave to their master. Resist romanticizing your life before Jesus or a season with fewer giants. Slavery is never better.

4. GOD PROMISED US.

God has promised you, through Jesus' words, that he will always be with you (Matthew 28:20). The valley of doubt will inevitably come, but you will not face the giants alone. Jesus will be with you. In Matthew 28, during Jesus' commissioning of the disciples after his resurrection, he promises to be with the people who follow him, to the end of the age. We can trust God's promises.

5. GO GET THE LAND.

You can move forward in confidence. Valley or not, God is with you, leading you and making a way for you to become a person of depth, wisdom, and courage. That's the potential of all your valleys of doubt—here, God is inviting you to grow deep roots of faith. Trust God with your giant-sized doubts so that you can enjoy the fruit in the valley.

Use this journaling space to process what you are learning.

Ask yourself how these truths impact your relationship with God and with others.

What is the Holy Spirit bringing to your mind as actionable next steps in your faith journey?

▼

▼

▼

FACING YOUR BATTLES WITH COURAGE AND CONVICTION

VALLEY OF KISHON:
WHERE DEBORAH AND JAEL DEFEAT THEIR ENEMY

SCRIPTURE: JUDGES 4–5

PART 1

CONTEXT

If talk of self-harm or substance abuse causes you emotional pain, consider coming back to part 1 at a different time or skipping this section altogether and rejoining us in part 2.

Before you begin your study, we will start with the context of the story we are about to read together: the setting, both cultural and historical; the people involved; and where our passage fits in the larger setting of Scripture. All these things help us make sense of what we're reading. Understanding the context of a Bible story is fundamental to reading Scripture well. Getting your bearings before you read will enable you to answer the question *What am I about to read?*

I HAVE FEW REGRETS IN LIFE, but all of them involve avoiding conflict. At the top of my "biggest regrets" list is a moment when I chose to run from a spiritual battle because I was afraid and embarrassed.

A group of prayer warriors and I were in a car, driving around our city, seeking God's direction on where to stop next to minister. Sheepishly, I mentioned that my dad could really use prayer and maybe we should drive a few extra miles to his home and check on him. Everyone in the car said that sounded like a good plan, but I panicked. They would be too close to home, quite literally.

What those folks didn't know was that my dad was losing his battle with untreated mental illness and substance abuse. I knew an intervention might be his only hope, but I didn't want to rock the boat. If we arrived unannounced at my dad's house, I imagined he would be accommodating in the moment only to save face and then turn around later to scold me for letting people in.

You know when you stomp down on the trash to get it to fit in the trash bin for pickup day? That's what I was doing spiritually in that car. I stuffed and stomped down the Holy Spirit's prodding and tried to make light of my suggestion.

"Never mind," I said. "Let's forget about it."

They tried to reason with me, but I lied through my teeth and said we should just head on back to the church and go our separate ways. So we did.

I didn't think of the car ride again until driving to the ICU to visit my dad after his suicide attempt.

He passed a few weeks later.

I know my dad's death is not my fault. I don't carry any lingering guilt about his decisions. Navigating the grief cycle, with a licensed professional counselor, has taught me as much. But I still wrestle with my lack of courage and conviction in that car ride. What I've come to realize is that my dad and I were fighting different battles. He was battling for his life in a deep valley of shame. I was having trouble facing my own battles in a valley of fear and insecurity.

You know the moments in your life that have shaped who you are and where you are going? That car ride did that for me. I want to be the kind of Christian who faces my battles with courage and conviction. I don't want to be afraid to pray ever again.

Does that resonate with you? Well, I have good news for us both. The Bible has a lot to say about the valleys we find ourselves in—and with that, a vision for choosing to stay when things get hard.

In our next valley, we're going to study two women—two of my *favorite* women, Deborah and Jael. They both stand their ground in the Valley of Kishon to defeat the enemy. Both women could have avoided conflict, but instead they show us how to step forward with courage and confidence.

Deborah's and Jael's stories are found in the book of Judges in the Old Testament. Judges chronicles the history of God's people under the rule of judges—Deborah

(Judges 4–5), Gideon (Judges 6–8), and Samson (Judges 13–16), to name a few. All these leaders came before the monarchy was set up in Israel.

The book of Judges records the depressing cycle of the Israelites' rebellion against God. Every time they reject God's plan, they launch into a downward spiral:

- rebelling against God by doing what is right in their own eyes,
- falling into oppression under evil foreign powers,
- crying out to God for help,
- being rescued by God, and
- entering a season of national peace.

This cycle continues throughout the book of Judges and only gets worse and worse. It's terrifying, actually. If Judges were a movie, it would be a horror film for sure.

Living in a time when all Israel was self-destructing, Deborah stands out as an exemplary judge and Jael is named "most blessed of women" (Judges 5:24). Deborah, the only woman to serve in judgeship over the nation of Israel, led God's people with wisdom and courage. In addition to her national influence, Deborah held the unique function of both fiery judge and authoritative prophet—speaking on behalf of God.[1] Similar to a king or queen, Deborah directed the military, too. Deborah was not God's plan B. She was an indispensable asset, chosen by God to lead.

Jael secured the victory in a battle between God's people and their enemy, the Canaanites. How? She drove a tent peg through the skull of Sisera, the Canaanite army commander. Yup. If that sounds gruesome to you, you're picturing the scene accurately. My friend Kaitlyn jokes that if she ever writes a book on biblical womanhood, the cover will showcase a bloody tent peg to honor the fierceness and courage of this particular woman.

You're about to read the summary of Deborah's reign as Israel's judge and of the battle between the Canaanites and the people of God in the Kishon Valley. My hope and prayer is that you will connect this valley to some of your own valleys in life. Maybe you feel like you're fighting a losing battle or hiding from your enemy. Take heart. Deborah and Jael show us that we are not the only ones needing backup . . . and that God gives us the boldness to trust that he'll come through.

1. **PERSONAL CONTEXT: What is going on in your life right now that might impact how you understand this Bible story?**

2. **SPIRITUAL CONTEXT: If you've never studied this Bible story before, what piques your curiosity? If you've studied this passage before, what impressions and insights do you recall? What problems or concerns might you have with the passage?**

PART 2

SEEING

Seeing the text is vital if we want the heart of the Scripture passage to sink in. We read slowly and intentionally through the text with the context in mind. As we practice close, thoughtful reading of Scripture, we pick up on phrases, implications, and meanings we might otherwise have missed. Part 2 includes close Scripture reading and observation questions to empower you to answer the question *What is the story saying?*

1. **Read Judges 4:1-23 while filling out the boxes in the outside margin. As you read, list what you learn about the characters in this story.**

4 Again the Israelites did evil in the eyes of the LORD, now that Ehud was dead. ² So the LORD sold them into the hands of Jabin king of Canaan, who reigned in Hazor. Sisera, the commander of his army, was based in Harosheth Haggoyim. ³ Because he had nine hundred chariots fitted with iron and had cruelly oppressed the Israelites for twenty years, they cried to the LORD for help.

⁴ Now Deborah, a prophet, the wife of Lappidoth, was leading Israel at that time. ⁵ She held court under the Palm of Deborah between Ramah and Bethel in the hill country

> King Jabin of Canaan:

Sisera:

Deborah:

Barak:

of Ephraim, and the Israelites went up to her to have their disputes decided. [6] She sent for Barak son of Abinoam from Kedesh in Naphtali and said to him, "The LORD, the God of Israel, commands you: 'Go, take with you ten thousand men of Naphtali and Zebulun and lead them up to Mount Tabor. [7] I will lead Sisera, the commander of Jabin's army, with his chariots and his troops to the Kishon River and give him into your hands.'"

[8] Barak said to her, "If you go with me, I will go; but if you don't go with me, I won't go."

[9] "Certainly I will go with you," said Deborah. "But because of the course you are taking, the honor will not be yours, for the LORD will deliver Sisera into the hands of a woman." So Deborah went with Barak to Kedesh. [10] There Barak summoned Zebulun and Naphtali, and ten thousand men went up under his command. Deborah also went up with him.

[11] Now Heber the Kenite had left the other Kenites, the descendants of Hobab, Moses' brother-in-law, and pitched his tent by the great tree in Zaanannim near Kedesh.

[12] When they told Sisera that Barak son of Abinoam had gone up to Mount Tabor, [13] Sisera summoned from Harosheth Haggoyim to the Kishon River all his men and his nine hundred chariots fitted with iron.

[14] Then Deborah said to Barak, "Go! This is the day the LORD has given Sisera into your hands. Has not the LORD gone ahead of you?" So Barak went down Mount Tabor, with ten thousand men following him. [15] At Barak's advance, the LORD routed Sisera and all his chariots and army by the sword, and Sisera got down from his chariot and fled on foot.

¹⁶ Barak pursued the chariots and army as far as Harosheth Haggoyim, and all Sisera's troops fell by the sword; not a man was left. ¹⁷ Sisera, meanwhile, fled on foot to the tent of Jael, the wife of Heber the Kenite, because there was an alliance between Jabin king of Hazor and the family of Heber the Kenite.

¹⁸ Jael went out to meet Sisera and said to him, "Come, my lord, come right in. Don't be afraid." So he entered her tent, and she covered him with a blanket.

¹⁹ "I'm thirsty," he said. "Please give me some water." She opened a skin of milk, gave him a drink, and covered him up.

²⁰ "Stand in the doorway of the tent," he told her. "If someone comes by and asks you, 'Is anyone in there?' say 'No.'"

²¹ But Jael, Heber's wife, picked up a tent peg and a hammer and went quietly to him while he lay fast asleep, exhausted. She drove the peg through his temple into the ground, and he died.

²² Just then Barak came by in pursuit of Sisera, and Jael went out to meet him. "Come," she said, "I will show you the man you're looking for." So he went in with her, and there lay Sisera with the tent peg through his temple—dead.

²³ On that day God subdued Jabin king of Canaan before the Israelites.

JUDGES 4:1-23

Jael:

Several elements in this story position Deborah as a second Moses. Both Deborah and Moses resisted the oppression of evil rulers, led God's people to victory against the enemy, ruled as judges over God's people, and experienced victory in valleys flooded with water.²

DEBORAH AS THE SECOND MOSES

Moses	Deborah
Moses' enemy was Pharaoh of Egypt, an evil and oppressive ruler. (Exodus 1:8-14)	Deborah's enemy was King Jabin of Canaan, an evil and oppressive ruler. (Judges 4:1-2)
Moses was a judge for God's people. (Exodus 18:13-16)	Deborah was a judge for God's people. (Judges 4:4-5)
God caused the water in the Valley of the Red Sea to sweep over the Egyptians. (Exodus 14:26-28)	God caused the water in the Valley of Kishon to sweep over the Canaanites. (Judges 5:20-21)
Moses experienced victory in the Valley of the Red Sea. (Exodus 14:26-31)	Deborah experienced victory in battle in the Valley of Kishon (Judges 4:7, 14, 23)
Moses sang a song about the victory. (Exodus 15:1-18)	Deborah sang a song about the victory. (Judges 5)

2. **Read Judges 5:1, 19-27 and draw a squiggly line under every mention of Kishon Valley water.**

5 On that day Deborah and Barak son of Abinoam sang. . . .

> ¹⁹ "Kings came, they fought,
>> the kings of Canaan fought.
>
> At Taanach, by the waters of Megiddo,
>> they took no plunder of silver.
>
> ²⁰ From the heavens the stars fought,
>> from their courses they fought against Sisera.
>
> ²¹ The river Kishon swept them away,
>> the age-old river, the river Kishon.
>>
>> March on, my soul; be strong!
>
> ²² Then thundered the horses' hooves—
>> galloping, galloping go his mighty steeds.
>
> ²³ 'Curse Meroz,' said the angel of the LORD.
>> 'Curse its people bitterly,

because they did not come to help the LORD,
  to help the LORD against the mighty.'

24 "Most blessed of women be Jael,
  the wife of Heber the Kenite,
  most blessed of tent-dwelling women.
25 He asked for water, and she gave him milk;
  in a bowl fit for nobles she brought him curdled milk.
26 Her hand reached for the tent peg,
  her right hand for the workman's hammer.
She struck Sisera, she crushed his head,
  she shattered and pierced his temple.
27 At her feet he sank,
  he fell; there he lay.
At her feet he sank, he fell;
  where he sank, there he fell—dead."

JUDGES 5:1, 19-27

3. **According to Judges 5:21, how were the nine hundred Canaanite chariots defeated?**

Deborah was not chosen and used by God because a good man was lacking in Israel. Rather, she was in her own right a woman of valor, a faithful prophet, and nationally recognized judge in her time (4:4-5), who supplemented her own limited gifts and calling by choosing a strong counterpart—a complement, if you please—to partner with her in rescuing Israel from a national crisis. Barak's insistence that she accompany him should be understood as no less than an appropriate plea for the presence of God. He implicitly recognized Deborah's seasoned wisdom and vital connection with God's will and word.[3]

Ron Pierce, "Deborah: Only When a Good Man Is Hard to Find?," in *Vindicating the Vixens*

If Deborah is like a second Moses, the imagery of the nine hundred Canaanite chariots being swept away in the Kishon Valley is like that of Pharaoh's army being swept away by the Red Sea.

4. According to Judges 5:24, what title does Jael hold among all women?

Jael is like the Proverbs 31 woman meets Wonder Woman or a Wakandan Dora Milaje. As the most blessed of women, Jael sets an example that should help us all broaden our perspective of what a godly woman looks like. Yes, God honors and celebrates the meek and mild who are devoted to him. But he also honors and celebrates women like Jael, who get their hands dirty with initiative-taking power moves as they advocate on behalf of God's people. Praise God for all the unique, treasured ways he fashions us to reflect his glory.

Both Deborah and Jael represent people who found courage because they trusted in God's power. I for one want to emulate their faith in God—and I think we could all learn a thing or two from them about defeating the enemy with trust in God's power.

PART 3

UNDERSTANDING

Now that we've finished a close reading of the Scriptures, we're going to spend some time on interpretation: doing our best to understand what God was saying to the original audience and what he's teaching us through the process. But to do so, we need to learn his ways and consider how God's Word would have been understood by the original audience before applying the same truths to our own lives. "Scripture interpretation" may sound a little stuffy, but understanding what God means to communicate to us in the Bible is crucial to enjoying a close relationship with Jesus. Part 3 will enable you to answer the question *What does it mean?*

AS THEY ENTERED THE VALLEY OF KISHON, the Canaanites seemed unbeatable. In Judges 4, the Lord made sure to include a statement of the power of King Jabin's army—nine hundred iron chariots. Embedded in this description is an assumption: The Canaanites could overpower anyone. No opposing army could contend with such horsepower. The imagery of iron chariots rolling over the Israelites may have haunted the thoughts of Barak and his army.

I felt that same dread of inevitable defeat when I hid my problems and resisted the Holy Spirit's leading. Why even try? Going in full-throttle flight mode felt safer. If I could close my eyes and look away from the lowest points in my life . . . somehow those problems might go away. That's why I relate to Barak in this story. He needed reassurance that Deborah would join the fight against Sisera. But what about Deborah—why was she so brave?

1. **Review Judges 4:14 and Judges 5:11. What do we see undergirding Deborah's confidence?**

The Scriptures point us to at least two reasons for her bravery. First, Deborah fought with courage because she was sure that God would deliver the Canaanites into Barak's hands in the Valley of Kishon. She says as much in Judges 4:6-7. Some translations of the verse quote Deborah as saying, "Hasn't the Lord the God of Israel commanded . . . ?" Her determination was rooted in believing God's message to his people. Maybe she assigned such faith to God's directives because she was used to receiving and dispensing his truth as Israel's judge. Whatever the case may be, I want to be more like Deborah when it comes to the valleys in my life, taking God at his word. You probably do too.

> God arranged the forces of nature and the details of the campaign so that the Israelites won a crushing victory.[4]
>
> Richard D. Patterson, "The Song of Deborah," in *Tradition and Testament: Essays in Honor of Charles Lee Feinberg*

The second reason Deborah fought the Canaanites with conviction is because she believed that God had gone before her army in battle and secured the victory through his supernatural power (Judges 4:14). She asked Barak this question: "Has not the LORD gone ahead of you?" The question is rhetorical, but it begs an answer. Yes. Of course God has gone before the victors. Though that's easier said than trusted.

We've talked before about the symbolic meaning of valleys in Scripture: They are places where our faith is tested. That's how both valleys we've studied together so far, the Valley of Eshkol and the Valley of Kishon, are connected.

THE VALLEYS OF ESHKOL AND KISHON

The Valley of Eshkol (Numbers 13–14)	The Valley of Kishon (Judges 4–5)
The Valley of Eshkol represents a place where our doubts test our faith in God.	The Valley of Kishon represents a place where our battles test our confidence in God.
The Valley of Eshkol is where Caleb, one of Moses' spies, scouted the Promised Land.	The Valley of Kishon is where Deborah and Jael defeated the Canaanite army.
Because the Israelites doubted God, they suffered forty years of wandering and testing in the desert.	Because of Deborah and Jael's courage and conviction, the Israelites experienced forty years of peace in the land.
The Valley of Eshkol was fertile ground.	The Valley of Kishon was a battleground.
Caleb's faith in God rested on God being with them in the valley.	Deborah's faith in God rested on God being ahead of them in battle.
Caleb said: *God said so.*	Deborah said: *Did God not say?*

Valleys can be fertile ground *and* battlegrounds—places where our faith and confidence in God are tested *and* can flourish. Maybe you need to hear that. The places of testing in your life are not all good or all bad. The tension you and I hold when we are in valleys of testing is enough to strain anyone's faith muscles. But remember: The exercise of faith and doubt is making your faith stronger.

2. **What would Deborah and Jael's victory in the Valley of Kishon mean to the Israelites? How might this have impacted their faith in God?**

3. What does their story show us about God?

MAKING CONNECTIONS

An important part of understanding the meaning of a Bible passage is getting a sense of its place in the broader storyline of Scripture. When we make connections between different parts of the Bible, we get a glimpse of the unity and cohesion of the Scriptures.

Deborah is never mentioned in the New Testament by name, but I think we have good reason to assume she is alluded to in Hebrews 11. Sometimes this passage of Scripture is referred to as the "Hall of Faith."

4. Read Hebrews 11:23-34 and Hebrews 12:1-2 and circle the names of the people in the "Hall of Faith."

23 By faith Moses' parents hid him for three months after he was born, because they saw he was no ordinary child, and they were not afraid of the king's edict.
24 By faith Moses, when he had grown up, refused to be known as the son of Pharaoh's daughter. 25 He chose to be mistreated along with the people of God rather than to enjoy the fleeting pleasures of sin. 26 He regarded disgrace for the sake of Christ as of greater value than the treasures of Egypt, because he was looking ahead to his reward. 27 By

faith he left Egypt, not fearing the king's anger; he persevered because he saw him who is invisible. ²⁸ By faith he kept the Passover and the application of blood, so that the destroyer of the firstborn would not touch the firstborn of Israel.

²⁹ By faith the people passed through the Red Sea as on dry land; but when the Egyptians tried to do so, they were drowned.

³⁰ By faith the walls of Jericho fell, after the army had marched around them for seven days.

³¹ By faith the prostitute Rahab, because she welcomed the spies, was not killed with those who were disobedient.

³² And what more shall I say? I do not have time to tell about Gideon, Barak, Samson and Jephthah, about David and Samuel and the prophets, ³³ who through faith conquered kingdoms, administered justice, and gained what was promised; who shut the mouths of lions, ³⁴ quenched the fury of the flames, and escaped the edge of the sword; whose weakness was turned to strength; and who became powerful in battle and routed foreign armies.

HEBREWS 11:23-34

12 Therefore, since we are surrounded by such a great cloud of witnesses, let us throw off everything that hinders and the sin that so easily entangles. And let us run with perseverance the race marked out for us, ² fixing our eyes on Jesus, the pioneer and perfecter of faith. For the joy set before him he endured the cross, scorning its shame, and sat down at the right hand of the throne of God.

HEBREWS 12:1-2

In verse 32, the author of Hebrews refers to "the prophets," and I believe that would have included Deborah. Deborah, who faced her battle against Sisera with courage and conviction, stands in our "cloud of witnesses."

5. Deborah led Israel to victory because of where she fixed her eyes. How does this connect to what we read in Hebrews 12?

If you feel ensnared by fear and the impulse to back down, remember: As we run our race, we can keep our eyes on Jesus and our ears open to the cheers coming from the cloud of witnesses. Maybe Deborah is cheering for you now—"Keep going!!!"

▼ ▼ ▼

Let's check back in on our Valleys Storyline.

THE VALLEYS STORYLINE OF SCRIPTURE

Location	Scripture	Protagonist
Valley of Eshkol	Numbers 13–14	Caleb
Valley of Kishon	Judges 4–5	Deborah
Valley of Elah	1 Samuel 17	David
Valley of Death	Psalm 23	the psalmist
Valley of Dry Bones	Ezekiel 37	Israel

Antagonist	Giants	Meaning
Canaanites	giants (the Anakim) living in the Promised Land	a valley where you can choose to trust
Canaanites	a giant-sized army: nine hundred iron chariots among King Jabin's forces	a valley where you can choose to face your battles with courage and conviction
Philistines	Goliath, a Philistine giant	a valley where you can choose to stay brave when the odds are against you
unsafe people and the depths of hardship	the giants of threat and danger	a valley where you can choose to follow the Good Shepherd through many dangers
Babylonian exile	the giants of hopelessness and death	a valley where you can choose to let God resurrect your hope

1. What valley are you walking through? How does this lesson remind you of God's presence in your valley?

2. What did you learn about God's character in this lesson?

3. How should these truths shape your faith community and change you?

RESPONDING

The purpose of Bible study is to help you become more Christlike; that's why part 4 will include journaling space for your reflection on and responses to the content and a blank checklist for actionable next steps. You'll be able to process what you're learning so that you can live out the concepts and pursue Christlikeness. Part 4 will enable you to answer the questions *What truths is this passage teaching?* and *How do I apply this to my life?*

ONE OF MY MAIN PROBLEMS when I'm in a valley battle is that I ignore God's presence. When I was sitting in that car in the watershed moment I described in part 1, I believed that even with the help of all the prayer warriors on the ride we would get nowhere with my dad.

What I hope to carry with me the next time I need to face a spiritual fight is that God is not only with me but also going *before me* into battle. I suspect you and I both long for more courage and conviction in valleys of testing. We are in this together, and our victorious God is ahead of us, leading the way, making a path forward and securing our victory. As we grow together in our confidence, here are some ways we can respond to the Valley of Kishon story.

1. FACE YOUR BATTLES.

You could turn around and run away from the battle in your valley. I certainly have experience going that route. But your problems are going to catch up with you. I know that facing off with our enemy sounds terrifying, but we cannot participate in God's victory if we don't enter the battle. You might be fighting to save your marriage, advocating for a special-needs child, battling for truth in a ministry context, or living with integrity in an industry that doesn't care about the common good. Whatever your fight, stay in it. We see from Deborah and Jael that showing up is half the battle. The rest is up to the Lord.

2. FIGHT WITH COURAGE.

Your valley might be so low that it brings you down with it. Your valley could be tempting you to act in ways incongruent with the character of Christ. If you are struggling with a short temper, resentment, disillusionment, or meanness, check yourself. That's not courage—it's the language of pain. Deborah and Jael show us a different way to fight. Courageous battles won't have you stoop to the lowest common denominator; instead, fighting with courage means trusting God with the outcome.

3. FIGHT WITH CONVICTION.

We can step into the battle, carrying the conviction of our God, who goes before us. In the same way God promised Deborah he would defeat the Canaanites, Jesus promises this to you:

- Jesus is preparing a place for you in his presence (John 14:1-4).
- Jesus will not leave you as an orphan; he is going to come back to be with us again (John 14:18).
- The Holy Spirit will teach you everything you need to know and remind you of Jesus' teachings (John 14:26).
- The enemy has no power over Jesus (John 14:30).

Use this journaling space to process what you are learning.

Ask yourself how these truths impact your relationship with God and with others.

What is the Holy Spirit bringing to your mind as actionable next steps in your faith journey?

▼

▼

▼

STAYING BRAVE WHEN THE ODDS ARE AGAINST YOU

**VALLEY OF ELAH:
WHERE DAVID FIGHTS GOLIATH**

SCRIPTURE: 1 SAMUEL 17

CONTEXT

Before you begin your study, we will start with the context of the story we are about to read together: the setting, both cultural and historical; the people involved; and where our passage fits in the larger setting of Scripture. All these things help us make sense of what we're reading. Understanding the context of a Bible story is fundamental to reading Scripture well. Getting your bearings before you read will enable you to answer the question *What am I about to read?*

HARRIET TUBMAN was a small, frail Black woman in a time when her gender and race made it extremely difficult for her to gain autonomy or agency. But she wouldn't back down. She stood toe-to-toe with the Goliath-sized evil of chattel slavery, helping smuggle African Americans out of slaveholding states and to freedom. She had escaped her own slave owners in Maryland and fled more than a hundred miles on foot, by herself, to freedom in Philadelphia. Her escape almost killed her, but Harriet lived and then spent the rest of her life freeing other slaves.

Harriet Tubman "made 19 trips into the South and escorted over 300 slaves to freedom" over the course of a decade. She boasted to Frederick Douglass that she "never lost a single passenger."[1] Her unrelenting passion and fortitude shocked even the most committed abolitionists.

How did Harriet stay brave?

Harriet was a devoted Christian woman who believed she heard God's voice.

She was convinced that his presence guided her on each of her nineteen trips into enemy territory, attributing her safety and that of her passengers to God's protection. Nothing rattled her.

After Harriet completed her last rescue mission, she served as a spy, scout, and leader in the Union army until the Civil War was over. According to the National Women's History Museum, she was the first African American woman to serve in the military.[2]

Leading abolitionist John Brown wrote that Harriet was "one of the . . . bravest persons on this continent."[3] I believe it. We should put Harriet Tubman's picture next to the dictionary's definition of *brave*.

Harriet should have died at a young age after suffering terrible abuse at the hands of her slave masters. She should have died in her escape. She should have died during any one of her nineteen rescue missions. The odds were against her every step of the way.

I wonder if you've ever felt like the odds are against you, too.

- ▾ You've been given a medical diagnosis with no cure. You feel like you, or someone you love, is living on borrowed time.
- ▾ You are the first in your family with aspirations to break the cycle of poverty, go to college, or own a home. You feel like trailblazing is a losing battle but one worth fighting.
- ▾ You are a person of color defying the odds of systemic injustice and the demonic stronghold of racism.

Whatever giant you face, maybe bravery feels too hard, too exhausting. Maybe what you're facing seems impossible and you need a miracle. And if you aren't currently in a valley that requires staying brave, you will be soon—opposition is part of the human condition. Whatever your odds, you will find encouragement and boldness in the Valley of Elah.

In our previous lesson, we got to know Deborah, an outlier among Israel's judges. Judgeship, as a way of governance, was largely an epic failure—most of the judges did not lead in a way that reflected God's values the way Deborah did.

God's people grew tired of corrupt judges and asked for a new form of government: a monarchy.

In the Old Testament books of 1 and 2 Samuel, 1 and 2 Kings, and 1 and 2 Chronicles, we learn that the Israelite monarchy had its advantages—but didn't come close to God's kingship. The Israelite monarchy created seasons of stability where the people of God were obedient to his commands and cared for by their king, but ultimately the system failed as leadership failed. As all forms of government do, the monarchy exposed that the people of God needed the King of all kings to rule with love and justice.

Of all the Israelite kings, King David was the best-known ruler of Israel. David wasn't born a royal. He was the baby of his family and grew up as a lowly shepherd tending his flocks. If you are not familiar with King David's rise to power, let me tell you that the whole story is fascinating, and you should check it out. But we're going to zoom in on one part in particular: an encounter David had with a giant named Goliath (1 Samuel 17).

What you're about to read is a story about David staying brave when the odds were against him and his people. He found himself facing Goliath in the Valley of Elah, which was a place of great opposition and difficulty. Things looked bleak in the Valley of Elah, but David wasn't distracted by the army around him or the might of the giant Goliath—his focus was on the strength of the God he served.

1. **PERSONAL CONTEXT: What is going on in your life right now that might impact how you understand this Bible story?**

2. **SPIRITUAL CONTEXT: If you've never studied this Bible story before, what piques your curiosity? If you've studied this passage before, what impressions and insights do you recall? What problems or concerns might you have with the passage?**

PART 2

SEEING

Seeing the text is vital if we want the heart of the Scripture passage to sink in. We read slowly and intentionally through the text with the context in mind. As we practice close, thoughtful reading of Scripture, we pick up on phrases, implications, and meanings we might otherwise have missed. Part 2 includes close Scripture reading and observation questions to empower you to answer the question *What is the story saying?*

1. **Read 1 Samuel 17:1–50 and fill in the boxes in the margin to note who is speaking in the paragraph.**

17 Now the Philistines gathered their forces for war and assembled at Sokoh in Judah. They pitched camp at Ephes Dammim, between Sokoh and Azekah. ² Saul and the Israelites assembled and camped in the Valley of Elah and drew up their battle line to meet the Philistines. ³ The Philistines occupied one hill and the Israelites another, with the valley between them.

⁴ A champion named Goliath, who was from Gath, came out of the Philistine camp. His height was six cubits and a span. ⁵ He had a bronze helmet on his head and wore a coat

of scale armor of bronze weighing five thousand shekels; [6] on his legs he wore bronze greaves, and a bronze javelin was slung on his back. [7] His spear shaft was like a weaver's rod, and its iron point weighed six hundred shekels. His shield bearer went ahead of him.

[8] Goliath stood and shouted to the ranks of Israel, "Why do you come out and line up for battle? Am I not a Philistine, and are you not the servants of Saul? Choose a man and have him come down to me. [9] If he is able to fight and kill me, we will become your subjects; but if I overcome him and kill him, you will become our subjects and serve us." [10] Then the Philistine said, "This day I defy the armies of Israel! Give me a man and let us fight each other." [11] On hearing the Philistine's words, Saul and all the Israelites were dismayed and terrified.

[12] Now David was the son of an Ephrathite named Jesse, who was from Bethlehem in Judah. Jesse had eight sons, and in Saul's time he was very old. [13] Jesse's three oldest sons had followed Saul to the war: The firstborn was Eliab; the second, Abinadab; and the third, Shammah. [14] David was the youngest. The three oldest followed Saul, [15] but David went back and forth from Saul to tend his father's sheep at Bethlehem.

[16] For forty days the Philistine came forward every morning and evening and took his stand.

[17] Now Jesse said to his son David, "Take this ephah of roasted grain and these ten loaves of bread for your brothers and hurry to their camp. [18] Take along these ten cheeses to the commander of their unit. See how your brothers are and bring back some assurance from them. [19] They are with Saul and all the men of Israel in the Valley of Elah, fighting against the Philistines."

Goliath

²⁰ Early in the morning David left the flock in the care of a shepherd, loaded up and set out, as Jesse had directed. He reached the camp as the army was going out to its battle positions, shouting the war cry. ²¹ Israel and the Philistines were drawing up their lines facing each other. ²² David left his things with the keeper of supplies, ran to the battle lines and asked his brothers how they were. ²³ As he was talking with them, Goliath, the Philistine champion from Gath, stepped out from his lines and shouted his usual defiance, and David heard it. ²⁴ Whenever the Israelites saw the man, they all fled from him in great fear.

²⁵ Now the Israelites had been saying, "Do you see how this man keeps coming out? He comes out to defy Israel. The king will give great wealth to the man who kills him. He will also give him his daughter in marriage and will exempt his family from taxes in Israel."

²⁶ David asked the men standing near him, "What will be done for the man who kills this Philistine and removes this disgrace from Israel? Who is this uncircumcised Philistine that he should defy the armies of the living God?"

²⁷ They repeated to him what they had been saying and told him, "This is what will be done for the man who kills him."

²⁸ When Eliab, David's oldest brother, heard him speaking with the men, he burned with anger at him and asked, "Why have you come down here? And with whom did you leave those few sheep in the wilderness? I know how conceited you are and how wicked your heart is; you came down only to watch the battle."

²⁹ "Now what have I done?" said David. "Can't I even speak?" ³⁰ He then turned away to someone else and brought up the same matter, and the men answered him as

before. ³¹ What David said was overheard and reported to Saul, and Saul sent for him.

³² David said to Saul, "Let no one lose heart on account of this Philistine; your servant will go and fight him."

³³ Saul replied, "You are not able to go out against this Philistine and fight him; you are only a young man, and he has been a warrior from his youth."

³⁴ But David said to Saul, "Your servant has been keeping his father's sheep. When a lion or a bear came and carried off a sheep from the flock, ³⁵ I went after it, struck it and rescued the sheep from its mouth. When it turned on me, I seized it by its hair, struck it and killed it. ³⁶ Your servant has killed both the lion and the bear; this uncircumcised Philistine will be like one of them, because he has defied the armies of the living God. ³⁷ The LORD who rescued me from the paw of the lion and the paw of the bear will rescue me from the hand of this Philistine."

Saul said to David, "Go, and the LORD be with you."

³⁸ Then Saul dressed David in his own tunic. He put a coat of armor on him and a bronze helmet on his head. ³⁹ David fastened on his sword over the tunic and tried walking around, because he was not used to them.

"I cannot go in these," he said to Saul, "because I am not used to them." So he took them off. ⁴⁰ Then he took his staff in his hand, chose five smooth stones from the stream, put them in the pouch of his shepherd's bag and, with his sling in his hand, approached the Philistine.

⁴¹ Meanwhile, the Philistine, with his shield bearer in front of him, kept coming closer to David. ⁴² He looked David over and saw that he was little more than a boy, glowing with health and handsome, and he despised him. ⁴³ He said to David, "Am I a dog, that you come at me with sticks?"

And the Philistine cursed David by his gods. ⁴⁴ "Come here," he said, "and I'll give your flesh to the birds and the wild animals!"

⁴⁵ David said to the Philistine, "You come against me with sword and spear and javelin, but I come against you in the name of the LORD Almighty, the God of the armies of Israel, whom you have defied. ⁴⁶ This day the LORD will deliver you into my hands, and I'll strike you down and cut off your head. This very day I will give the carcasses of the Philistine army to the birds and the wild animals, and the whole world will know that there is a God in Israel. ⁴⁷ All those gathered here will know that it is not by sword or spear that the LORD saves; for the battle is the LORD's, and he will give all of you into our hands."

⁴⁸ As the Philistine moved closer to attack him, David ran quickly toward the battle line to meet him. ⁴⁹ Reaching into his bag and taking out a stone, he slung it and struck the Philistine on the forehead. The stone sank into his forehead, and he fell facedown on the ground.

⁵⁰ So David triumphed over the Philistine with a sling and a stone; without a sword in his hand he struck down the Philistine and killed him.

1 SAMUEL 17:1-50

2. **Using 1 Samuel 17:3-4 as a reference, draw the battle formation at the Valley of Elah.**

3. **Based on 1 Samuel 17:3-7, what feelings do you think the Israelite army were processing? Check all that apply.**

☐ terror

☐ insecurity

☐ overwhelm

☐ intimidation

☐ insignificance

☐ defeat

If you are fearful, insecure, overwhelmed, intimidated, discouraged, and defeated, know this: You are in a battle, in a valley. This low point in your life might feel like war—even if it's not a visible war with a tangible enemy, like the army of Israel faced.

I can only imagine that as Goliath taunted the Israelites with his towering strength, inching toward the battle lines with his shield bearer, the men who were lined up in formation felt as though they would faint. Dismayed and terrified, the Israelites must have been frozen by fear.

King Saul should have led the men into battle and inspired some confidence, but he didn't. Isn't that sometimes part of our valley struggle too? Sometimes leaders fail to go first and we are left to manage the crisis without direction.

4. **According to 1 Samuel 17:16, how many days did Goliath take his stand?**

☐ ten

☐ twenty

☐ thirty

☐ forty

Remember—the number forty in the Bible represents a time long enough to test our faith.

THE NUMBER FORTY IN THE BIBLE

Who Was Being Tested	Length of the Test
Caleb, the spies, and the Israelites (Numbers 13–14)	In the Valley of Eshkol, Caleb and the rest of Moses' spies spent *forty days* scouting the Promised Land. After the Israelites rejected Caleb's report, they spent *forty years* wandering in the desert because of their unbelief.
Deborah, Jael, and the Israelites (Judges 4–5)	In the Valley of Kishon, after Deborah and Jael secured victory for Israel, the Israelites experienced *forty years* of peace in the land.
David and the Israelites (1 Samuel 17)	In the Valley of Elah, the giant Philistine warrior, Goliath, took his stand against the Israelites for *forty days*.
Jesus (Matthew 4)	Jesus was tested in the wilderness for *forty days* before his victory over temptation.

Usually we find ourselves in a valley for a long enough time to bring us down and cause us to question God. There is no magic in the number forty, but its use in Scripture does suggest that it symbolizes the significant time needed for us to dig deep in our faith.

5. **List the reasons David's brother Eliab and King Saul both believed David was unlikely to succeed against Goliath (1 Samuel 17:28-33):**

▼

▼

▼

▼

▼

David was too young and too inexperienced. He had no armor and no shield bearer. And last but not least—David wasn't a giant. From an earthly perspective, David was a goner.

6. List the reasons David believed he could defeat Goliath (1 Samuel 17:45–47).

▼

▼

▼

▼

When I sense that I'm freezing up in battle, knees locked, about to faint from fear, I think of David's bravery. David's courage in the Valley of Elah is a clarion call to you and to me: We are not asked to win in our own strength but to use what little we have and to trust God with the victory. The battle is the Lord's, after all.

PART 3

UNDERSTANDING

Now that we've finished a close reading of the Scriptures, we're going to spend some time on interpretation: doing our best to understand what God was saying to the original audience and what he's teaching us through the process. But to do so, we need to learn his ways and consider how God's Word would have been understood by the original audience before applying the same truths to our own lives. "Scripture interpretation" may sound a little stuffy, but understanding what God means to communicate to us in the Bible is crucial to enjoying a close relationship with Jesus. Part 3 will enable you to answer the question *What does it mean?*

WHEN WE ARE at one of our lowest lows in life, we are in a valley—but by God's grace, that valley can become one of the places where our faith will grow the deepest. Over and over in Scripture we have seen that valleys are where God's people face down doubts, cowardice, and death-defying odds to find trust, courage, conviction, and bravery. Why does God cement these stories in our faith history? Why repeat the valley location? Why so many valley battles?

I think he is making a point. God knows that our lives are filled with ups and downs. In our valleys, we face giant-sized enemies that threaten to crush our confidence in God. But he wants us to know that we can survive and thrive in our darkest moments. When our circumstances dip into scary situations, you and I can borrow the faith of people like Caleb, Deborah, Jael, and David.

1. **Which element of the valleys we've studied thus far is most impactful or surprising to you?**

2. **What have you learned about the God of the valleys?**

MAKING CONNECTIONS

An important part of understanding the meaning of a Bible passage is getting a sense of its place in the broader storyline of Scripture. When we make connections between different parts of the Bible, we get a glimpse of the unity and cohesion of the Scriptures.

After David's victory in the Valley of Elah, he won several other important battles and became known as the warrior-king of Israel. His rise to the throne started in obscurity as a shepherd tending flocks of sheep, but he grew into a king who shepherded the people of Israel. He did so imperfectly—but nonetheless, David's role foreshadowed King Jesus.

Both King David and King Jesus were born in Bethlehem, and both were known as shepherds and kings. In John 10:11, Jesus says, "I am the good shepherd. The good shepherd lays down his life for the sheep."

At the end of the book of Hebrews, the author reminds Christians that part of the joy of being a Christ follower is being shepherded by the Good Shepherd, Jesus.

3. **Read Hebrews 13:20-21, circling every reference to Jesus as a shepherd and Christ followers being his sheep.**

    ²⁰ Now may the God of peace, who through the blood of the eternal covenant brought back from the dead our Lord Jesus, that great Shepherd of the sheep, ²¹ equip you with everything good for doing his will, and may he work in us what is pleasing to him, through Jesus Christ, to whom be glory for ever and ever. Amen.

    HEBREWS 13:20-21

4. **What role does sacrifice play in the life of the shepherd?**

5. **How does Jesus as the Good Shepherd perfect and expand on David as a shepherd, both of sheep and of the Kingdom?**

You and I are living in the middle of a cosmic battle between good and evil, and the enemy is sending out giants to intimidate us. Much like David in the Valley of Elah, we have to stand our ground and let the Lord fight our battles. With Jesus, our Good Shepherd and the King of kings, the ultimate victory is sure.

Let's check back in on Valleys Storyline.

THE VALLEYS STORYLINE OF SCRIPTURE

Location	Scripture	Protagonist
Valley of Eshkol	Numbers 13–14	Caleb
Valley of Kishon	Judges 4–5	Deborah
Valley of Elah	1 Samuel 17	David
Valley of Death	Psalm 23	the psalmist
Valley of Dry Bones	Ezekiel 37	Israel

Antagonist	Giants	Meaning
Canaanites	giants (the Anakim) living in the Promised Land	a valley where you can choose to trust
Canaanites	a giant-sized army: nine hundred iron chariots among King Jabin's forces	a valley where you can choose to face your battles with courage and conviction
Philistines	Goliath, a Philistine giant	a valley where you can choose to stay brave when the odds are against you
unsafe people and the depths of hardship	the giants of threat and danger	a valley where you can choose to follow the Good Shepherd through many dangers
Babylonian exile	the giants of hopelessness and death	a valley where you can choose to let God resurrect your hope

1. What valley are you walking through? How does this lesson remind you of God's presence in your valley?

2. What did you learn about God's character in this lesson?

3. How should these truths shape your faith community and change you?

RESPONDING

The purpose of Bible study is to help you become more Christlike; that's why part 4 will include journaling space for your reflection on and responses to the content and a blank checklist for actionable next steps. You'll be able to process what you're learning so that you can live out the concepts and pursue Christlikeness. Part 4 will enable you to answer the questions *What truths is this passage teaching?* and *How do I apply this to my life?*

YOU'VE SEEN THIS MOVIE, RIGHT? An underdog takes the field against an undefeatable enemy. On the sidelines, the naysayers get loud as the odds seem insurmountable. The crowds chant against Rocky when he defeats the Russian in *Rocky IV.* The Sith Lord taunts Rey that she is "nothing" and just a scavenger in *Star Wars: The Rise of Skywalker.* In *The Dark Knight Rises,* Bane threatens Batman with terrifying, muffled bully tactics. And *Karate Kid* fans will remember the shout heard across all TV screens: "Put him in a body bag, Johnny!" According to the silver screen, it's a key part of the battle: The enemy begins to speak, taunting the underdog.

We see it first all the way back in 1 Samuel 17 in the Valley of Elah. David is clearly the underdog. The naysayers aren't just on the Philistine side—his own brother and King Saul doubt his motives and his ability. And then, as David steps onto the field, Goliath starts to speak.

I imagine Goliath's voice matching his giant stature—that his words were amplified as if through a megaphone. And how did Goliath use his booming words during the fight? He intimidated and insulted David, defying God by defying his people.

Perhaps someone in your life has spoken harmful words over you. Maybe you've been told that you're nothing, worthless, a mess, hopeless. Your bullies weaponize your deficiencies or conjure up lies. Whatever their tactics, their words can be a broken record in your mind, replaying *you're too much*—or *not enough* or *alone* or *unwanted*.

Take heart. David knows your pain. He shows us what it is to ignore the shouts and lies and trust God for the victory. With God's power, you can too. Here are three ways you can stay brave when your naysayers get loud.

1. STAY BRAVE WHEN NAYSAYERS TRY TO INTIMIDATE YOU.

One of the taunts Goliath voices to David is "Why do you come out and line up for battle? Am I not a Philistine, and are you not the servants of Saul?" (1 Samuel 17:8). Goliath tempted his opponents to believe they were nothing. *Who do they think they are? Don't they know that the great Philistine warriors always win?*

Stay brave when your naysayers get loud with lies about your identity. You know who you are: a child of the Most High God.

2. STAY BRAVE WHEN NAYSAYERS TRY TO DEFY GOD.

Goliath also dares to defy God by defying God's people, a prideful move on his part. He says, "This day I defy the armies of Israel!" (1 Samuel 17:10). Goliath challenged the Israelites to do something everyone had deemed impossible—win a fight against a giant. Goliath didn't understand that their God was far more powerful than he would ever be.

Stay brave when your naysayers get loud about impossibilities. Nothing is impossible for your God.

3. STAY BRAVE WHEN NAYSAYERS TRY TO INSULT YOU.

Goliath says to David, "Am I a dog, that you come at me with sticks?" (1 Samuel 17:43). Goliath bullied David, trying to get him to believe that his weapons were useless and pitiful. What use is a stick against a giant? Maybe that's how you feel about your education, experience, or power. You feel like you're carrying tiny twigs up against bronze armor.

Stay brave when your naysayers get loud with put-downs. Your best weapon is to follow God into battle.

▼ ▼ ▼

Every single one of us lacks something we need to win our fight against the enemy. David lacked experience, height, armor, a shield bearer, the support of his family, and the example of his king. What do you lack? Energy, money, contacts, health, wisdom? It wouldn't be a valley battle if the stakes weren't high and the probability of victory low. Your valleys are where God shows up. Your valleys are where God is strong, no matter how weak you feel. And he will go before you, even when you lack something you think is crucial to staying in the fight.

Use this journaling space to process what you are learning.

Ask yourself how these truths impact your relationship with God and with others.

What is the Holy Spirit bringing to your mind as actionable next steps in your faith journey?

▼

▼

▼

RESISTING FEAR WHEN YOUR LIFE BOTTOMS OUT

**VALLEY OF DEATH:
WHERE GOD COMFORTS SCARED PEOPLE**

SCRIPTURE: PSALM 23

CONTEXT

Before you begin your study, we will start with the context of the story we are about to read together: the setting, both cultural and historical; the people involved; and where our passage fits in the larger setting of Scripture. All these things help us make sense of what we're reading. Understanding the context of a Bible story is fundamental to reading Scripture well. Getting your bearings before you read will enable you to answer the question *What am I about to read?*

"I QUIT A JOB to help my friend as she died."

Evelyn's comments in Bible study were unexpected, to say the least. Our online small group had been talking about experiences that taught us to trust God, and that's when Evelyn began to share her story. I sat on the edge of my seat, leaning closer to the screen to listen.

Several years before, a dear friend of Evelyn's had entered the final, painful stages of terminal cancer. Evelyn took a radical step: She quit her job so that she could take her friend to doctor's appointments and simply spend time at her side before she passed. Incredibly, after her friend went to be with the Lord, Evelyn was able to quickly get her job back with a raise and a promotion. There was no question in Evelyn's mind—God had provided what she needed so that she could help her friend. As she wrapped up her story, Evelyn bore witness to God's loving-kindness and mercy.

Evelyn's intentional unemployment and sacrificial care, coupled with God's provision, tell a powerful story in their own right. But here's what you don't know: that Evelyn *herself* is battling cancer for a second time. Thanks to Zoom, I get to stay in Evelyn's orbit while she takes every precaution to protect her health. Her gorgeous, smiling, hopeful face appears on my screen on Wednesday nights, her head crowned with a beanie because of chemo and radiation.

Evelyn is a spiritual giant. She's beloved by church members and known by her dearest friends as faithful and generous. When Evelyn's talking to you, you feel like the only person on planet earth, like her only mission in life is to remind you of God's love.

Evelyn has walked through this lesson's valley several times. She's got frequent flier miles under the shadow of death; she's breaking Fitbit records in the pits of cancer. If you want to know how to resist fear when life bottoms out, Evelyn is your person.

Whether it's you or your loved one who is sinking down into the dust of hardship, crying out from the depths of the soul, this lesson is for you. Whether you or your loved one are on the brink of death or facing imminent danger, the crisis in your life is not a surprise to God. Life's darkest experiences are valleys where Jesus travels with us. You will see that clearly in Psalm 23, our passage for this week's study.

What you are about to read is a Hebrew poem written by King David. You don't need to know anything about King David's story to know that he shares a lot in common with fellow valley travelers like Evelyn. David's poem in Psalm 23 is proof enough.

The book of Psalms is a collection of 150 songs in poetic form. For organizational purposes, these rhythmic literary pieces are grouped into five sections, or books.

> Psalm 23 is a convincing witness that God is our Shepherd, that God is the Shepherd who preserves us, accompanies us, and rules us. He doesn't just create us and turn us loose to make the best we can of it. He doesn't just let us fend for ourselves until we die and are hauled before the judgment seat for an accounting of our conduct. He is the Shepherd who guides us in our wanderings and sustains us in our fugitive lives.[1]
>
> Eugene H. Peterson,
> *As Kingfishers Catch Fire*

Five Books of Psalms[2]	
Book I	Psalms 1–41
Book II	Psalms 42–72
Book III	Psalms 73–89
Book IV	Psalms 90–106
Book V	Psalms 107–150

Unless you are a rapper, musician, or poet, reading a psalm has its challenges. Like all poetry, the language is not precise. The imagery, allusions, and metaphors hold within them meaning beyond the words themselves. Many times, the sacred poetry paints a picture in our minds or brings shape to an intangible concept in our souls. Psalm 23, the topic of this lesson, is no different. In six short verses, the twenty-third psalm encapsulates staying hopeful when your life is at risk.

Scholar Ellen T. Charry describes Psalm 23 this way:

We cling to life through it when the angel of death stalks our path. We recite it to face down danger and fear when they lunge out in the dark. We sing it as we long to live in the mercy that we need to dwell in the house of the Lord every day of our life. Such is the comforting eloquence of the Twenty-Third Psalm.[3]

If you ask someone in your life their favorite psalm, they'll probably rank Psalm 23 at the top of the list. It's likely the most beloved, well-known, memorized song in the Scriptures. Psalm 23 is a part of a grouping of songs in the Bible designated as "trust" psalms[4] or "confidence" psalms.[5] In light of what I've learned from my friend Evelyn, this makes complete sense. How can a song about the terrors of our darkest valleys be an expression of trust and confidence? Because those dark valleys are where our God walks beside us.

TRUST PSALMS[7]

Psalm 23
Psalm 91
Psalm 121
Psalm 125
Psalm 131

The twenty-third psalm was my mainstay in college when my sibling attempted suicide and my parents went through bankruptcy. In my thirties, the twenty-third psalm was my plumb line when my father-in-law was in quadruple bypass surgery and when my mom had a cancer diagnosis. The poem you are about to study has functioned as my first line of defense when I am scared to death *and* scared of death. My prayer is that Psalm 23 becomes the song you sing when life "plumbs the anguished depths of the heart."[8] Embedded in this poem is the kind of unwavering trust you and I both need when we walk through death valleys—divorce, cancer, homelessness, depression, domestic violence, and any other cavern of life we may find ourselves in.

1. **PERSONAL CONTEXT: What is going on in your life right now that might impact how you understand this Bible story?**

2. **SPIRITUAL CONTEXT: If you've never studied this Bible passage before, what piques your curiosity? If you've studied this passage before, what impressions and insights do you recall? What problems or concerns might you have with the passage?**

SEEING

Seeing the text is vital if we want the heart of the Scripture passage to sink in. We read slowly and intentionally through the text with the context in mind. As we practice close, thoughtful reading of Scripture, we pick up on phrases, implications, and meanings we might otherwise have missed. Part 2 includes close Scripture reading and observation questions to empower you to answer the question *What is the story saying?*

---

1. **Read Psalm 23 and draw or describe how the poet's images appear in your imagination.**

¹ The Lᴏʀᴅ is my shepherd;
I have what I need.

² He lets me lie down in green pastures;
he leads me beside quiet waters.

³ He renews my life;
he leads me along the right paths
for his name's sake.

⁴ Even when I go through the darkest valley,

I fear no danger,

for you are with me;

your rod and your staff—they comfort me.

⁵ You prepare a table before me

in the presence of my enemies;

you anoint my head with oil;

my cup overflows.

⁶ Only goodness and faithful love will pursue me

all the days of my life,

and I will dwell in the house of the LORD

as long as I live.

PSALM 23, CSB

One of my favorite Bible commentators, Ben Witherington III, summarizes the four functions of the Psalms this way:

> (1) as material for singing in the temple and elsewhere; (2) as Scripture to be read in the temple and later in the synagogue (and memorized); (3) as prayers that could be recited privately or in corporate worship; and (4) as a source for teaching and preaching.[9]

If Psalm 23 can serve us in these different ways, how could a poem about God's care and power to deliver in the Valley of Death be a help to the body of Christ?

2. If Psalm 23 were sung at church, what kind of music would you envision accompanying the poem? How would it help the body of Christ?

3. If Psalm 23 were used as liturgy (a script for public worship) in the church, something we memorize to recite, what kind of emotions do you think it would evoke? When would be a good time to recite this poem?

4. If Psalm 23 became a prayer you repeated to yourself, when you would pray this prayer in your personal life?

5. If Psalm 23 were the Scripture reading at church, the passage in the lectionary, or a topic you were given to teach or preach on, what kind of stories would you share alongside this poem?

PART 3

UNDERSTANDING

Now that we've finished a close reading of the Scriptures, we're going to spend some time on interpretation: doing our best to understand what God was saying to the original audience and what he's teaching us through the process. But to do so, we need to learn his ways and consider how God's Word would have been understood by the original audience before applying the same truths to our own lives. "Scripture interpretation" may sound a little stuffy, but understanding what God means to communicate to us in the Bible is crucial to enjoying a close relationship with Jesus. Part 3 will enable you to answer the question *What does it mean?*

CLOSE, STEADY READINGS of Psalm 23 seem most effective for understanding this soulful song. That's why I've organized this part of your study so that you read one verse at a time. For your viewing pleasure, and maybe for a few giggles, I've included pictures of my own drawings from part 2. I hope this inspires you to draw even if you have no talent for drawing. (I am the poster child for lack of artistic skills.) Additionally, you'll see a quote or two from a Bible scholar that I know will help unpack the rich words of each verse. Last, I'll offer you some insights that come to mind as I process King David's ode to Jesus, the Good Shepherd.

▼ ▼ ▼

VERSE 1

The LORD is my shepherd;
I have what I need.

1. What do you think the psalmist means when he says that the Lord is a shepherd?

SCHOLARS' QUOTES

Metaphorical sheep appear as hapless dolts in many scriptural references.
They are stupid, helpless animals and the most easily domesticated
for food, especially since they are relatively small and easily managed.
They are unable to sense danger to protect themselves . . . or care for
themselves very well . . . and need someone to guide them.[10]

Sheep are notorious for their stupidity. Left to themselves they wander
aimlessly into danger.[11]

INSIGHTS

This phrase—*I have what I need*—changed my life. When scarcity thinking and
a fixed mindset keep us from trusting God or cause us to become self-protective
in fear of potential disappointment, let's reflect on the truth that we have what
we need.

VERSE 2

He lets me lie down in green pastures;
he leads me beside quiet waters.

2. What do you think the psalmist means when he says that God leads people to green pastures and quiet waters?

SCHOLAR'S QUOTE

[The Hebrew words translated as "he makes me lie down" or "he lets me lie down" denote] the active agency of the shepherd in seeking out an environment in which the sheep may thrive.[12]

INSIGHTS

Sometimes I wonder where God is leading me. Maybe you feel similarly. *How is this path in my life going to get me somewhere safe?* You and I can trust that when the Good Shepherd guides us, he is taking us to places where we can rest and be replenished.

▼   ▼   ▼

He renews my life;
he leads me along the right paths
for his name's sake.

3.   What do you think the psalmist means when he says that the Lord renews his life?

SCHOLAR'S QUOTE

The image is of someone who has almost stopped breathing and is revived, brought back to life.[13]

INSIGHTS

My soul is comforted every time I consider that God's pathways are connected to his character. Because God is love, I can trust that every path he's designed for my life is connected to his love for me. The path may be winding, but I don't ever have to question where the Good Shepherd is leading: for my good and for his glory.

VERSE 4

> Even when I go through the darkest valley,
> I fear no danger,
> for you are with me;
> your rod and your staff—they comfort me.

4. What do you think the psalmist means when he says that he's going through the darkest valley?

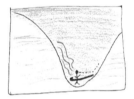

SCHOLAR'S QUOTE

It is noteworthy that it is precisely in the middle of the crisis (*the darkest valley*) that the psalm shifts from creedal affirmations about God to trusting prayer to God. It is in moments of crisis that the Lord moves from an abstract concept (a *he* about whom one has memorized doctrinal statements) to a living God with whom one has a relationship (a *you* in whom one trusts, to whom one speaks, on whom one can rely).[14]

INSIGHTS

King David's confession challenges me because I'm scared of everything. Some of my closest friends call me Scaredy-Kat. What keeps me from being frozen by fear is knowing that God is with me. That's why I choose to lead afraid, learn afraid, try afraid. I am not doing it alone.

VERSE 5

> You prepare a table before me
> in the presence of my enemies;
> you anoint my head with oil;
> my cup overflows.

5. What do you think the psalmist means when he says that the Lord prepares a table before him in the presence of his enemies?

SCHOLAR'S QUOTE

How is this possible when there are enemies around? Only God can make this possible. With God it is possible to sleep even in the midst of the battle ([Psalm] 3:5); so also one can celebrate in the midst of opposition.[15]

INSIGHTS

Until very recently, I was confused about this image: feasting with Christ in the presence of enemies. How could our cups run over with joy if we are surrounded by unsafe people, those who would undermine or attack us? As I reflected on the psalm, suddenly it became clear: We are at peace and filled with joy because our focus is not on our enemies but on the presence of Christ.

▼ ▼ ▼

Only goodness and faithful love will pursue me
all the days of my life,
and I will dwell in the house of the LORD
as long as I live.

6. What do you think the psalmist means when he says that goodness and faithful love will pursue him all the days of his life?

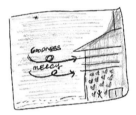

SCHOLAR'S QUOTE

Psalm 23 is a convincing witness that God is our Shepherd, that God is the Shepherd who preserves us, accompanies us, and rules us. He doesn't just create us and turn us loose to make the best we can of it. He doesn't just let us fend for ourselves until we die and are hauled before the judgment seat for an accounting of our conduct. He is the Shepherd who guides us in our wanderings and sustains us in our fugitive lives.[16]

INSIGHTS

The imagery of Jesus, the Good Shepherd, pursuing me gets me every time. He is not idle or passive. He is moving ever forward, ensuring that his goodness and faithful love reach my life. Jesus chases me down to bless and encourage me.

An important part of understanding the meaning of a Bible passage is getting a sense of its place in the broader storyline of Scripture. When we make connections between different parts of the Bible, we get a glimpse of the unity and cohesion of the Scriptures.

In addition to being a key image in many psalms, shepherds are important characters in the narrative of Jesus' birth and the focus of several parables Jesus teaches in the Gospels. The imagery of God as our Good Shepherd in Psalm 23 reverberates throughout the Scriptures like an echo in a ravine.

One of the parts of the Bible that haunts me the most is the passage containing the chilling words of condemnation from God to his people spoken through the prophet Ezekiel in Ezekiel 34. In this passage, God is described as a shepherd who will not stand by and let his sheep be neglected, unprotected, abused, or starved to death. Notice with me the harsh rebuke God gives unjust caretakers.

7. **Read Ezekiel 34:1-6. Use the lines that follow to list the charges brought against the evil shepherds.**

34 The word of the LORD came to me: ² "Son of man, prophesy against the shepherds of Israel. Prophesy, and say to them, 'This is what the Lord GOD says to the shepherds: Woe to the shepherds of Israel, who have been feeding themselves! Shouldn't the shepherds feed their flock? ³ You eat the fat, wear the wool, and butcher the fattened animals, but you do not tend the flock. ⁴ You have not strengthened the weak, healed the sick, bandaged the injured, brought back the strays, or sought the lost. Instead, you have ruled them with violence and cruelty. ⁵ They were scattered for lack of a shepherd; they became food for all the wild animals when they were scattered. ⁶ My flock went astray on all the mountains and every high hill. My flock was scattered over the whole face of the earth, and there was no one searching or seeking for them.'"

EZEKIEL 34:1-6, CSB

What are the charges against the evil shepherds?

▼

▼

▼

▼

▼

▼

8. **Read Ezekiel 34:11-16. Use the lines following the verses to list the promises God makes as the Good Shepherd.**

11 "'This is what the Lord GOD says: See, I myself will search for my flock and look for them. 12 As a shepherd looks for his sheep on the day he is among his scattered flock, so I will look for my flock. I will rescue them from all the places where they have been scattered on a day of clouds and total darkness. 13 I will bring them out from the peoples, gather them from the countries, and bring them to their own soil. I will shepherd them on the mountains of Israel, in the ravines, and in all the inhabited places of the land. 14 I will tend them in good pasture, and their grazing place will be on Israel's lofty mountains. There they will lie down in a good grazing place; they will feed in rich pasture on the mountains of Israel. 15 I will tend my flock and let them lie down. This is the declaration of the Lord GOD. 16 I will seek the lost, bring back the strays, bandage the injured, and strengthen the weak, but I will destroy the fat and the strong. I will shepherd them with justice.'"

EZEKIEL 34:11-16, CSB

The promises of the Good Shepherd:

▼

▼

▼

▼

▼

▼

▼

▼

The kings in Jerusalem failed to act as protective shepherds in leading their people, and that was the reason the people of God would be exiled for a time. The whole nation would be punished for the monarchs' failures.[17] We should not miss the warning for us in this. How do we care for the vulnerable people we encounter? God takes matters of justice seriously.

Correspondingly, I hope you are encouraged by the tangible ways your Good Shepherd cares for his sheep. He rescues us, gathers us, tends to us, and makes sure we are taken care of.

9. What are some specific ways God acts as the Good Shepherd?

Because I read the Bible Christologically, or with Jesus in mind, I believe that Psalm 23 and Ezekiel 34 are both speaking prophetically about Jesus as the Good Shepherd. Something Jesus says in the book of John points us to this truth.

John was a beloved disciple and friend of Jesus who followed him during his earthly ministry and witnessed his life, death, and resurrection. Thanks to John's faithfulness to Christ, we have his perspective on Jesus' teachings and miracles in the Gospel of John. Throughout John's Gospel, Jesus that proves he is God. Jesus doesn't say the words *I am God*, but he poetically and clearly equates himself to God the Father with enough authority that the Jews demand his crucifixion. Jesus was crucified because of this seemingly blasphemous way of speaking about his equality with and identity as God. One example of this is in John 10, when Jesus says he is the Good Shepherd.

10. As you read John 10:11-18, underline every mention of a shepherd.

¹¹ "I am the good shepherd. The good shepherd lays down his life for the sheep. ¹² The hired hand, since he is not the shepherd and doesn't own the sheep, leaves them and runs away when he sees a wolf coming. The wolf then snatches and scatters them. ¹³ This happens because he is a hired hand and doesn't care about the sheep.

¹⁴ I am the good shepherd. I know my own, and my own know me, ¹⁵ just as the Father knows me, and I know the Father. I lay down my life for the sheep. ¹⁶ But I have other sheep that are not from this sheep pen; I must bring them also, and they will listen to my voice. Then there will be one flock, one shepherd. ¹⁷ This is why the Father loves me, because I lay down my life so that I may take it up again. ¹⁸ No one takes it from me, but I lay it down on my own. I have the right to lay it down, and I have the right to take it up again. I have received this command from my Father."

JOHN 10:11-18, CSB

Life in the desert for both Shepherd and sheep is no soft, sun-drenched idyll on a south sea island. It is menaced by the dark shadows of the beast-infested valley. The threats to life are all around, but the presence of the Shepherd guides and leads, dispersing the threats.[18]

Eugene H. Peterson, *As Kingfishers Catch Fire*

When Jesus announced to his followers that he was "the good shepherd" (John 10:14), I don't think they understood him to mean that he was a gentle, kind shepherd who would be nice to the sheep. They lived in shepherd country and knew something of the realities of a shepherd's life. Being a good shepherd meant taking the risk of life against beasts, robbers, and murderers (and they knew it).[19]

Eugene H. Peterson, *As Kingfishers Catch Fire*

Maybe like me, you need to be reminded that the God of the universe, the all-powerful, almighty King of all kings, is guarding your life. If you know Christ as Savior, you have a Good Shepherd who knows you and who laid down his life for you on the cross because he loves you. That God, that Savior, Jesus—*he* is who walks with you through the Valley of Death.

Let's check back in on our Valleys Storyline.

THE VALLEYS STORYLINE OF SCRIPTURE

Location	Scripture	Protagonist
Valley of Eshkol	Numbers 13–14	Caleb
Valley of Kishon	Judges 4–5	Deborah
Valley of Elah	1 Samuel 17	David
Valley of Death	Psalm 23	the psalmist
Valley of Dry Bones	Ezekiel 37	Israel

Antagonist	Giants	Meaning
Canaanites	giants (the Anakim) living in the Promised Land	a valley where you can choose to trust
Canaanites	a giant-sized army: nine hundred iron chariots among King Jabin's forces	a valley where you can choose to face your battles with courage and conviction
Philistines	Goliath, a Philistine giant	a valley where you can choose to stay brave when the odds are against you
unsafe people and the depths of hardship	the giants of threat and danger	a valley where you can choose to follow the Good Shepherd through many dangers
Babylonian exile	the giants of hopelessness and death	a valley where you can choose to let God resurrect your hope

1. What valley are you walking through? How does this lesson remind you of God's presence in your valley?

2. What did you learn about God's character in this lesson?

3. How should these truths shape your faith community and change you?

RESPONDING

The purpose of Bible study is to help you become more Christlike; that's why part 4 will include journaling space for your reflection on and responses to the content and a blank checklist for actionable next steps. You'll be able to process what you're learning so that you can live out the concepts and pursue Christlikeness. Part 4 will enable you to answer the questions *What truths is this passage teaching?* and *How do I apply this to my life?*

THE LAST TIME I recited Psalm 23 to myself was the day after my father died. My eyes looked like Muhammad Ali had been punching me all night, and my head pounded with a grief hangover. As I tried to muster energy to emerge from the hiddenness of my bed, I wished that the mattress would dip in the middle and swallow me into a place where I wouldn't have to face my first day without my dad. My only comfort came from the familiar words that I whispered hoarsely under my breath. This is the power of the sacred poem that is Psalm 23.

Rolf A. Jacobson describes this experience in his commentary on Psalm 23:

This is the true setting of the psalm: the existential space of being in the presence of something that is terrifying, a space in which every reflective human being finds himself or herself at some point, and a space in which, according to the witness of the poem, the Lord can also be found.[20]

My dad was gone, but Jesus was present. Ever by my side, hemming me in on his paths, following me with his goodness and mercy, Jesus stayed with me. You may find yourself in that place, needing these ancient words to remind you that you don't face pain and fear alone. Whatever ravine closes in around you, you have a Good Shepherd and a generous host who is with you, present to protect you and to provide for your every need. That's why the psalmist could say—in earnest—"I have what I need." He believed it to be true.

Receive the truths sung about in Psalm 23. Take these words to heart. We all walk through the Valley of Death many times in our lives. If you are not there right now, you may soon find yourself on that path. Resisting fear when life bottoms out has a lot to do with believing the following truths.

1. IT'S OKAY TO BE JESUS' NEEDY SHEEP; JESUS IS YOUR GOOD SHEPHERD.

Whether you value self-sufficiency or trend toward codependency, death valleys are a great equalizer when it comes to neediness. There are just some things you and I can't climb our way out of, even though we might try. That's why trying times are called "times of need." You and I need help when we are in the lowlands of life. You don't need to lift yourself up by your bootstraps or whistle someone down to help you up. You need a Good Shepherd—and you have one. Jesus is never so busy with his other needy sheep that he can't take care of you. In Luke 15:3-7, Jesus says that if he had a hundred sheep and one got lost, he would leave the ninety-nine to come find you.

If you struggle to believe you are worth your Good Shepherd's care, maybe you need to focus on the fact that he is good and can't be anything else. It's okay to be one of Jesus' needy sheep. The thing is, we *can't* be anything else. We are his sheep; he is the Shepherd. And not just any shepherd—he is the good one. You can count on his rod and staff to steer you along to safety. His goodness and mercy are chasing you down.

2. IT'S OKAY TO BE JESUS' WANDERING GUEST; JESUS IS YOUR GENEROUS HOST.

We hosted our church's worship team for lunch recently, and it wasn't until our guests left that my eight-year-old son sheepishly admitted that he'd directed one of our guests to use his own bathroom. My cringe affirmed his concerns. Mind you, I'd cleaned the guest bathroom. But Caleb reasoned that since the guest bathroom had been full when our guest had needed to "go potty," the alternative would do.

I imagined our guest wandering through a side of the house we rarely invite guests to view. She must have traveled over the piles of sprawled Legos, the squalor of stinky, post–sports practice socks, and the sticky misses of an elementary-age child's toilet. When I texted her about her visit to our only dirty bathroom, she replied with laughing emojis and commiseration. She, too, is a mom of elementary-age kids. She knew I would feel stressed about her seeing a bathtub covered in crayon marks. She admitted she felt a little lost on the way there. But she said that it was precious how Caleb had acted as the host of the house. Without me, my husband, or my mom around, Caleb made sure our guest had a place to use the restroom.

I think a lot of us feel like a wandering guest when it comes to the valley of shadows. We don't know our way around. We know we don't want to go the direction of darkness, and we try to keep our eyes straight ahead toward our destination—but ultimately, it's too dark to see our way forward. If that is you, and you feel out of your depth, know this: Jesus is a generous host. It brings him great joy to prepare a table for you where you will taste his provisions and inhale the fragrance of joy. When Jesus is your host, you leave the valley of shadows with more than you need.

Use this journaling space to process what you are learning.

Ask yourself how these truths impact your relationship with God and with others.

What is the Holy Spirit bringing to your mind as actionable next steps in your faith journey?

▼

▼

▼

RESURRECTING HOPE WHEN YOUR CONFIDENCE IN GOD IS LOST

VALLEY OF DRY BONES:
WHERE EZEKIEL PROPHESIES ISRAEL'S RESTORATION

SCRIPTURE: EZEKIEL 37

PART 1

CONTEXT

Before you begin your study, we will start with the context of the story we are about to read together: the setting, both cultural and historical; the people involved; and where our passage fits in the larger setting of Scripture. All these things help us make sense of what we're reading. Understanding the context of a Bible story is fundamental to reading Scripture well. Getting your bearings before you read will enable you to answer the question *What am I about to read?*

"SPIRITUALLY, I'M IN A DRY SPELL. I'm not flourishing at all. Honestly, my faith feels brittle, like one more loss and I might snap."

My friend responded to a direct message with total honesty—his ministry life had bottomed out. He went on to share that it wasn't just one thing; a litany of grievances had ground him down. The loss he grieved the most? He'd lost his confidence in God. This was no walk through a death valley—he was visiting the gravesites of church work. Dream after dream had been buried under church hurt and disillusionment.

As a guy, he's likely never received social-media ads about preventing osteoporosis, the weakening of bones. But as soon as he said the word *brittle*, I pictured the calcium supplements Instagram has been pushing into my feed. My pastor friend was suffering not with a weakening of bones but with a weakening of hope.

According to the Mayo Clinic, "osteoporosis causes bones to become weak and brittle—so brittle that a fall or even mild stresses such as bending over or coughing can cause a fracture" because "the creation of new bone doesn't keep up with the loss of old bone."[1] My friend's experience in ministry was similar. His weakened faith had left him vulnerable to any new ministry stress. Each disappointment, in its own right, was something rather mild, but in his weakened state it felt like a crack in his hope hemisphere.

His story and yours may share some similarities. It might not be ministry woes that get you down, but perhaps you keep losing battles in your valleys and your confidence in God has been shaken. Or maybe you know what it's like when God's company isn't a comfort anymore, when God's victories don't feel like wins, or when God's power seems to be thwarted. My pastor friend isn't the only one who shares your burdens. I, too, question why some death valleys become open graves and not memorials of victory.

Up until this point, the valleys we've studied together have been battlefields or the locations where shadows cast doubt on our future. In this lesson we're going to see a much darker kind of valley in Ezekiel 37. This valley is a graveyard—a place where Israelite warriors seem to be cursed. The Valley of Dry Bones, in Ezekiel 37, is a piece of imagery for a hopeless people—but it does not leave them there. In the middle of a graveyard, death is resurrected to new confidence in God.

If you have time to dig into Ezekiel's whole story, it's a fascinating read. For our purposes, I want to mention a few noteworthy aspects of Ezekiel's life and spend the bulk of our time exploring the Valley of Dry Bones. Ezekiel was the son of Buzi (Ezekiel 1:3), and he was a part of a tribe in Israel who served as priests. Ezekiel never got to fulfill his calling as a priest because he was a member of the group of God's people who were exiled from their land to enemy territory in Babylon.[2] If you know the pain that accompanies preparing and planning for a future that never comes to fruition, you are connected to Ezekiel's story and that of the people he ministered to. Even though he was a part of the Jerusalem priesthood, his entire ministry was performed outside of Israel. Right from the start, Ezekiel's life story is set up in a long, deep valley in Israel's history and represents the loss of his birthright calling before it began. All situational hardships pointed to unrealized dreams and disappointment.

At first glance (and without some digging into biblical commentaries), Ezekiel's behavior throughout the book he wrote is concerning at best. Sometimes he seems unhinged or even deranged. Sometimes when Ezekiel is obeying God he acts paranoid and erratic, which makes me wonder what his marriage was like. Scholars have a wide variety of explanations for Ezekiel's odd behavior, but I for one am going to accept it as a mystery.

As interesting as I find Ezekiel's life to be, what grabs my attention about his story is the group of deported people he was ministering to—the Israelites. The Jews Ezekiel prophesied to were distraught about being forced away from their home and grieving that they could not live the way God intended—worshiping God in the Jerusalem Temple. Put yourself in their shoes for a moment. You're supposed to be in your home, the land promised to you by God. Babylonian powers took you away from the life you wanted, denying you access to your city and the Temple of your God. Imagine how defeated you would feel.

Every person hearing Ezekiel's sermons or listening to his prophecies was likely "cynical, bitter, and angry" with God.[3] In the passage of Scripture we're going to study, Ezekiel's message grips my attention because I know all of us will, at some point, be knee-deep in the ashy ruins of hope deferred. You and the people listening to Ezekiel might share something in common—namely, a crisis of faith. Who among us doesn't start to question God's goodness when our prayers seem to be unanswered and his promises seem to go unkept? Which one of us doesn't tilt our head with suspicion when God seems to be sleeping on the job?

There is another layer to the Israelites' story. They were in this mess because of their own wrongdoing. They'd given themselves over to idolatry time and time again, resisting God's instructions for fidelity to him alone. This time, when they begged for more idols, he finally gave them what they wanted. One of the

> Because he displayed many bizarre actions, some have characterized Ezekiel as neurotic, paranoid, psychotic, or schizophrenic. However, his unusual behavior derives from his utter obedience to God. Ezekiel was gripped by the Spirit of God, had a profoundly theological perspective on contemporary historical events, and exhibited an unflinching determination to deliver the messages just as God gave them.[4]
>
> Daniel I. Block, *By the River Chebar*

consequences was displacement. I wonder if sandwiched between their bitterness and anger with God was a thick layer of shame.

You're going to see that the Valley of Dry Bones is filled with corpses . . . and yet it also becomes a place where resurrection is possible. If you know in full, or in part, what it's like to have your spiritual bones dried up, or to have your hope gone, or to feel cut off from your life source—Jesus—I'm convinced that your confidence in God will be revived in this lesson.

You're going to see life after death and land after exile.

You're going to hear ancient words of God that seem to meet you in your valley now.

You're going to see what God can do with dry bones and gravesites.

You're going to see that even when everything seems dead, our God is still a God of resurrection life.

1. **PERSONAL CONTEXT: What is going on in your life right now that might impact how you understand this Bible story?**

2. **SPIRITUAL CONTEXT: If you've never studied this Bible story before, what piques your curiosity? If you've studied this passage before, what impressions and insights do you recall? What problems or concerns might you have with the passage?**

SEEING

Seeing the text is vital if we want the heart of the Scripture passage to sink in. We read slowly and intentionally through the text with the context in mind. As we practice close, thoughtful reading of Scripture, we pick up on phrases, implications, and meanings we might otherwise have missed. Part 2 includes close Scripture reading and observation questions to empower you to answer the question *What is the story saying?*

1. **Read Ezekiel 37:1-14 and underline anytime you see Ezekiel using one of his five senses: sight, touch, sound, smell, or taste.**

37 The hand of the LORD was on me, and he brought me out by the Spirit of the LORD and set me in the middle of a valley; it was full of bones. ² He led me back and forth among them, and I saw a great many bones on the floor of the valley, bones that were very dry. ³ He asked me, "Son of man, can these bones live?"

I said, "Sovereign LORD, you alone know."

⁴ Then he said to me, "Prophesy to these bones and say to them, 'Dry bones, hear the word of the LORD! ⁵ This is what the Sovereign LORD says to these bones: I will make breath enter you, and you will come to life.

⁶ I will attach tendons to you and make flesh come upon you and cover you with skin; I will put breath in you, and you will come to life. Then you will know that I am the LORD.'"

⁷ So I prophesied as I was commanded. And as I was prophesying, there was a noise, a rattling sound, and the bones came together, bone to bone. ⁸ I looked, and tendons and flesh appeared on them and skin covered them, but there was no breath in them.

⁹ Then he said to me, "Prophesy to the breath; prophesy, son of man, and say to it, 'This is what the Sovereign LORD says: Come, breath, from the four winds and breathe into these slain, that they may live.'" ¹⁰ So I prophesied as he commanded me, and breath entered them; they came to life and stood up on their feet—a vast army.

¹¹ Then he said to me: "Son of man, these bones are the people of Israel. They say, 'Our bones are dried up and our hope is gone; we are cut off.' ¹² Therefore prophesy and say to them: 'This is what the Sovereign LORD says: My people, I am going to open your graves and bring you up from them; I will bring you back to the land of Israel. ¹³ Then you, my people, will know that I am the LORD, when I open your graves and bring you up from them. ¹⁴ I will put my Spirit in you and you will live, and I will settle you in your own land. Then you will know that I the LORD have spoken, and I have done it, declares the LORD.'"

EZEKIEL 37:1-14

2. **Look again at Ezekiel 37:1. What might Ezekiel have experienced with all five of his senses before the Lord started speaking?**

What did Ezekiel see when in the middle of the valley?

What might Ezekiel have smelled in the middle of the valley?

What did Ezekiel touch when in the middle of the valley?

What did Ezekiel hear when in the middle of the valley?

What might Ezekiel have tasted, if anything, when in the middle of the valley?

Ezekiel's vision of restoration is not simply a plan for a future physical Jerusalem. Rather, his vision is a heavenly exemplar that figured in the exilic life of the community.[5]

Dexter E. Callender Jr., "Exodus," in *The Africana Bible*

Everything grosses me out, so I'm rattled by this morbid scene in Ezekiel 37, where the prophet is standing in the middle of an open grave of dry bones. Would Ezekiel be breathing in bone dust and choking on the stench of death? *Ew.* Did the wind sweep up bone debris into his eyes and cause them to water? *I can't.* If he moved, did he hear the snap, crackle, and pop of bones? *Ick.* Imagining this moment in Ezekiel's life reminds me of the brittle bones Indiana Jones climbs over to seek his treasure, or the Marvel Avenger dust Thanos creates after mass murder—*it's too much for me to handle.*

3. **What does God say to the dry bones in Ezekiel 37:5?**

66   **99**

4. **How did God resurrect the dry bones in Ezekiel 37:4-10?**

5. **According to Genesis 2:7, how did God complete the creation of people?**

Whole books and academic journals have been written to connect the pieces of God's life-breathing creation activity throughout the Bible. From beginning to end, God is the Genesis Creator and Beginning Maker. He can breathe life into newly formed bodies or, in the case of Ezekiel 37, life into dead bodies to remake what death has destroyed. This is good news for those of us who can hear death knocking. This is good news for those of us mourning the burial of a dream.

6. **If you were there in the Valley of Dry Bones and heard the rattling sound of the bones coming together, what would you be thinking?**

    a. *What is happening?*

    b. *This is gross.*

    c. *I can't believe my eyes!*

    d. *Won't he do it!*

    e. *This makes sense.*

7. **Based on Ezekiel 37:11, who do the dry bones represent?**

    a. you

    b. me

    c. the people of Israel

8. **Based on Ezekiel 37:12, what does the Valley of Dry Bones represent?**

    a. a scary place

    b. the land of Israel

My husband, Aaron, nearly faints at the sight of blood. And I've already confessed that I can't stomach grossness. Between the two of us, we've warned our son, Caleb, that if he ever needs stitches, the whole family is going to be in a world of hurt. As I picture Ezekiel watching cracked and bare bones shaking out of their place in the valley and joining to tendons and skin, the gruesome imagery takes my breath away. Maybe that's part of God's point: Death is horrifying—and only he can revive us, with his breath.

Let us take away just one thing from this amazing text. The Israelites have done less than nothing to restore God's faith in them. He does not raise them from the dust because they have repented. He raises them from the dust because he is their God. This is the theme of Ezekiel.[6]

Fleming Rutledge, "Nothing More True," in *And God Spoke to Abraham*

PART 3

UNDERSTANDING

Now that we've finished a close reading of the Scriptures, we're going to spend some time on interpretation: doing our best to understand what God was saying to the original audience and what he's teaching us through the process. But to do so, we need to learn his ways and consider how God's Word would have been understood by the original audience before applying the same truths to our own lives. "Scripture interpretation" may sound a little stuffy, but understanding what God means to communicate to us in the Bible is crucial to enjoying a close relationship with Jesus. Part 3 will enable you to answer the question *What does it mean?*

ON MY MOTHER'S SIDE OF THE FAMILY, we observe Día de los Muertos, the Day of the Dead, as a way of honoring and celebrating our relatives who have passed. This two-day annual holiday is an opportunity to connect with relatives we cherish in our memories. Although my faith in Christ reorients the way I participate with my family on Día de los Muertos, I appreciate the rich heritage that seeks to understand the connection between life and death.

Most cultures have traditions around the concept of life after death. The Mesopotamian people living during Ezekiel's ministry had views on the afterlife as well. They believed that once a person died, proper burial was required for their spirit to "take their place among the dead."[7] If for some reason someone was left unburied after death, not only would they lose their place in the afterlife but they would also be assumed to be demonic. Remaining unburied after death was considered a curse in Ezekiel's day.[8]

When God chooses to use the gravesite of unburied Israelite soldiers as the setting to teach Ezekiel about resurrection, he is also showing God's people that, even if the Mesopotamians were right about the curse upon the unburied, the God of Israel breaks every curse with life after death—burial or not.

Maybe that's how the exiled Israelites felt about their longing for their land—maybe they felt like unburied fallen soldiers, cursed by God. Maybe that's how *you* feel, cursed by God. Here's what I would say to you now:

Cursed or not, buried or not—if you know Jesus as Savior, God's resurrection power cannot and will not be diminished or restrained in your life, ever.

Resurrection is your future, which I believe is God's point in the Valley of Dry Bones. God is giving Ezekiel and all the people listening to his sermons a vision for Israel's future. God is restoring hope lost. And he can do that for you, too. He does so through the resurrection of Jesus Christ.

1. **What thoughts and emotions do you imagine God's people had when they heard Ezekiel's sermons and vision about the Valley of Dry Bones?**

Like many OT prophecies, this one has multiple meanings and fulfilments. It communicates more than just the hope of Israel's return to the land. It is also a picture of those who are spiritually dead in sin who are brought to life by the Spirit through faith in Jesus. It also contains the hope of the resurrection for those who believe in him—those who die in Jesus will one day live again in a body he will recreate.[9]

Eliya Mohol, "Ezekiel," in *South Asia Bible Commentary*

2. What would the people have learned about God from the scene?

Fast forward to the New Testament, and you'll see that Ezekiel's prophecy in the
Valley of Dry Bones finds its ultimate fulfillment in Jesus' resurrection from the
dead. The Scriptures are clear: Jesus lived; he died on the cross; he was dead and
buried; and then on the third day he rose from the dead and the grave tomb was
empty. The whole of the Christian faith rests on Jesus' victory over death.

There are several different places I could point you to in the Bible to explore
Jesus' resurrection, but I'm partial to John's retelling in John 20.

3. As you read John 20:1-18, circle each occurrence of Mary's name:

20 Early on the first day of the week, while it was still dark, Mary
Magdalene went to the tomb and saw that the stone had been removed
from the entrance. ² So she came running to Simon Peter and the other
disciple, the one Jesus loved, and said, "They have taken the Lord out of
the tomb, and we don't know where they have put him!"

³ So Peter and the other disciple started for the tomb. ⁴ Both were
running, but the other disciple outran Peter and reached the tomb first.
⁵ He bent over and looked in at the strips of linen lying there but did not go
in. ⁶ Then Simon Peter came along behind him and went straight into the

tomb. He saw the strips of linen lying there, [7] as well as the cloth that had been wrapped around Jesus' head. The cloth was still lying in its place, separate from the linen. [8] Finally the other disciple, who had reached the tomb first, also went inside. He saw and believed. [9] (They still did not understand from Scripture that Jesus had to rise from the dead.) [10] Then the disciples went back to where they were staying.

[11] Now Mary stood outside the tomb crying. As she wept, she bent over to look into the tomb [12] and saw two angels in white, seated where Jesus' body had been, one at the head and the other at the foot.

[13] They asked her, "Woman, why are you crying?"

"They have taken my Lord away," she said, "and I don't know where they have put him." [14] At this, she turned around and saw Jesus standing there, but she did not realize that it was Jesus.

[15] He asked her, "Woman, why are you crying? Who is it you are looking for?"

Thinking he was the gardener, she said, "Sir, if you have carried him away, tell me where you have put him, and I will get him."

[16] Jesus said to her, "Mary."

She turned toward him and cried out in Aramaic, "Rabboni!" (which means "Teacher").

[17] Jesus said, "Do not hold on to me, for I have not yet ascended to the Father. Go instead to my brothers and tell them, 'I am ascending to my Father and your Father, to my God and your God.'"

[18] Mary Magdalene went to the disciples with the news: "I have seen the Lord!" And she told them that he had said these things to her.

JOHN 20:1-18

Jesus' resurrection story begins differently than Ezekiel's resurrection vision in the Valley of Dry Bones: Rather than the Lord calling Ezekiel to the valley, Mary Magdalene—one of Jesus' female disciples—comes to the garden tomb on her own initiative. But the scene feels ominous, much like Ezekiel's. Mary is knee-deep in a graveyard, disoriented and afraid. The stone covering the opening to Jesus' tomb has been rolled away, and Jesus' body is missing. In Ezekiel's story, the dead bodies in the Valley of Dry Bones are missing flesh, but in Jesus' resurrection story, all that's left of the dead body are the linen cloths he was buried in.

God asks Ezekiel a question about the dry bones: *Can these bones live?* In John 20, Mary Magdalene is asked several questions, one by two angels and more by Jesus himself. Both stories reveal that beneath these questions is a desire to dig into the existential questions below the surface. *Can I trust God?* Or *Can I trust God again?*

Ezekiel's answer to God's question is a nod to his sovereignty—only God knows if life is possible after death. When Jesus questions Mary and asks her why she is crying, she doesn't recognize him and supposes he is a gardener.

She wasn't right, but she wasn't wrong either. Jesus *is* the Cosmic Gardener. In his life, death, and resurrection, Jesus replants humanity back into the story of redemption, much as he replanted and restored Israel to their Promised Land in the Valley of Dry Bones.

In the same way God commissioned Ezekiel to prophesy to the people of Israel that their hope could be revived, Christ commissioned Mary Magdalene to tell her brothers of the resurrection she has witnessed: Jesus is alive.

Jesus' resurrection is the reason valleys do not defeat us. When he conquered death and proved his deity, he launched a revolution. In the book of 1 Peter, one of the New Testament authors summarizes why Jesus' resurrection means so much to Christians.

4. As you read 1 Peter 1:3-7, underline any mention or description of Christ's resurrection:

³ Praise be to the God and Father of our Lord Jesus Christ! In his great mercy he has given us new birth into a living hope through the resurrection of Jesus Christ from the dead, ⁴ and into an inheritance that can never perish, spoil or fade. This inheritance is kept in heaven for

you, ⁵ who through faith are shielded by God's power until the coming of the salvation that is ready to be revealed in the last time. ⁶ In all this you greatly rejoice, though now for a little while you may have had to suffer grief in all kinds of trials. ⁷ These have come so that the proven genuineness of your faith—of greater worth than gold, which perishes even though refined by fire—may result in praise, glory and honor when Jesus Christ is revealed.

1 PETER 1:3-7

Maybe you put your hope in the outcome that never materialized, the relationship that didn't last, the job opportunity that passed you by. I've lived through all these things myself. And because of that, I can admit that I'm guilty, often, of misplacing my trust and expectations on a future I can't completely control. Thankfully, Peter shows us what to do when we are ready to recenter our lives around the only unshakable hope. If your hope feels dead, I encourage you to turn your eyes toward Christ's resurrection. Christian hope is living.

5. **What are some of the things in your life that have not yet materialized? How has your capacity to hope been impacted by these unmet expectations or trials?**

6. **How does the Valley of Dry Bones story shift our understanding of resurrection?**

Write out 1 Peter 1:13:

When your hope has no pulse, set your hope completely on the grace to be brought to you when Christ returns. If Jesus rose, he will return. As sure as the Resurrection is the foundation of our faith, Christ's return is the solid ground for your confidence.

Let's check back in on our Valleys Storyline.

THE VALLEYS STORYLINE OF SCRIPTURE

Location	Scripture	Protagonist
Valley of Eshkol	Numbers 13–14	Caleb
Valley of Kishon	Judges 4–5	Deborah
Valley of Elah	1 Samuel 17	David
Valley of Death	Psalm 23	the psalmist
Valley of Dry Bones	Ezekiel 37	Israel

Antagonist	Giants	Meaning
Canaanites	giants (the Anakim) living in the Promised Land	a valley where you can choose to trust
Canaanites	a giant-sized army: nine hundred iron chariots among King Jabin's forces	a valley where you can choose to face your battles with courage and conviction
Philistines	Goliath, a Philistine giant	a valley where you can choose to stay brave when the odds are against you
unsafe people and the depths of hardship	the giants of threat and danger	a valley where you can choose to follow the Good Shepherd through many dangers
Babylonian exile	the giants of hopelessness and death	a valley where you can choose to let God resurrect your hope

1. What valley are you walking through? How does this lesson remind you of God's presence in your valley?

2. What did you learn about God's character in this lesson?

3. How should these truths shape your faith community and change you?

RESPONDING

The purpose of Bible study is to help you become more Christlike; that's why part 4 will include journaling space for your reflection on and responses to the content and a blank checklist for actionable next steps. You'll be able to process what you're learning so that you can live out the concepts and pursue Christlikeness. Part 4 will enable you to answer the questions *What truths is this passage teaching?* and *How do I apply this to my life?*

REFLECTING ON THE VALLEY OF DRY BONES has been, at times, an agonizing exercise for me. Yes, the hope of resurrection is the most encouraging news I've ever heard. Yes, I sensed the breath of God blowing on me as I studied and processed Ezekiel's prophecies. And yes, God's vision of my future lifted my spirits. The caverns of hopelessness don't rule me anymore. My confidence in God's timing, his purpose, and his ways has been renewed. And all because of God's resurrection power in the Valley of Dry Bones.

But the reassurance came at a cost. The price was placing myself in Ezekiel 37 long enough to absorb the bone-grinding setting, a graveyard. Though I was eager to move on to visions of the nation of Israel restored, and how Jesus fulfills this future perfectly, I paused instead.

The longer I reckoned with the mass grave of Israelite soldiers and haunting scenery of the Valley of Dry Bones, the more I pondered other people groups who have suffered unspeakable losses. I thought about the popular podcast *The Rise and Fall of Mars Hill* and the thousands of Christians referred to as "bodies behind the bus."[10] I reflected on American chattel slavery and the horrors Black Americans suffered when lynching was rampant. I reviewed history on the Holocaust in Germany and the Rwandan genocide.

The piles of dead bodies in the Valley of Dry Bones became symbolic of all the atrocities of history I bury six feet under my memory.

Let's not forget that Ezekiel had to stand on dry bones before seeing God breathe new life into resurrected bodies—this is the paradoxical way Ezekiel's story unfolds. Maybe that's how it goes for all of us. We hold in tension the beauty of resurrection against a backdrop of death. Because resurrection is only necessary if we go through death. We must face the weight and terror of death to behold the beauty of resurrection. The two are inextricably linked.

Whatever God stirred up in your soul through this lesson, know this: You can feel the burden of hardship while also being caught up in a joyful, hope-restoring move of God.

Here are two points to ponder as you respond to the Valley of Dry Bones:

1. YOU WILL COME BACK TO LIFE.

If you know Jesus as your Savior, then anything that feels lost or dead or lifeless will come back to life when Christ returns. This is a reality that awaits all Christians, and it is good news!

The apostle Paul puts it this way in one of his letters to the Christians in Corinth:

> 20 Christ has indeed been raised from the dead, the firstfruits of those who have fallen asleep. 21 For since death came through a man, the resurrection of the dead comes also through a man. 22 For as in Adam all die, so in Christ all will be made alive. 23 But each in turn: Christ, the firstfruits; then, when he comes, those who belong to him.
>
> 1 CORINTHIANS 15:20-23

Until then, Christ's resurrection power is available to you now in what I call microresurrections. You know that nagging, broken relationship you want reconciled? The wayward child, the opportunities lost, the wages stolen from you? You know the time you feel like you'll never get back? If it seems as good as dead, God can work a miracle now. But even if he doesn't, your future is still bright. When Christ comes back to remake the world, he's going to remake you, too.

2. YOU WILL SEE GOD'S PROMISES FULFILLED.

It might not be on this side of eternity, but you will see God's promises fulfilled. Every ache your heart has endured, every prayer left seemingly unanswered, every failure—all of it will find its completion in the new heaven and new earth. Christ is returning to resurrect his world. According to the Scriptures, when God recreates, he invites us to watch him do it. I wonder if that is what John alludes to in the book of Revelation:

21 Then I saw "a new heaven and a new earth," for the first heaven and the first earth had passed away, and there was no longer any sea. ² I saw the Holy City, the new Jerusalem, coming down out of heaven from God, prepared as a bride beautifully dressed for her husband. ³ And I heard a loud voice from the throne saying, "Look! God's dwelling place is now among the people, and he will dwell with them. They will be his people, and God himself will be with them and be their God. ⁴ 'He will wipe every tear from their eyes. There will be no more death' or mourning or crying or pain, for the old order of things has passed away."

⁵ He who was seated on the throne said, "I am making everything new!" Then he said, "Write this down, for these words are trustworthy and true."

REVELATION 21:1-5

Ezekiel's vision proves again that when life bottoms out, our valleys can become a place where our faith flourishes. And it serves as a reminder that a day is coming when all the wrongs in this world will be made right, all God's promises will be fulfilled, and all his dreams for your life will be realized.

Use this journaling space to process what you are learning.

Ask yourself how these truths impact your relationship with God and with others.

What is the Holy Spirit bringing to your mind as actionable next steps in your faith journey?

▼

▼

▼

As You Go

YOU DID IT. You dug into five valleys in the Bible:

- ▾ the Valley of Eshkol, where Moses' spies scouted the Promised Land;
- ▾ the Valley of Kishon, where Deborah and Jael defeated their enemy;
- ▾ the Valley of Elah, where David fought Goliath;
- ▾ the Valley of Death, where God comforts scared people; and
- ▾ the Valley of Dry Bones, where Ezekiel prophesied Israel's restoration.

With every valley, I hope God reminded you that he has made—and always will make—a way to be with you in the lowlands of life.

Whether it's a spiritual mountaintop or a valley of doubt, there's no mountain too high or valley too low to keep you away from his love.

PS: I've loved this time with you, and I hope you join me again for another journey in the **Storyline Bible Studies**.

THE VALLEYS STORYLINE OF SCRIPTURE

Location	Scripture	Protagonist
Valley of Eshkol	Numbers 13–14	Caleb
Valley of Kishon	Judges 4–5	Deborah
Valley of Elah	1 Samuel 17	David
Valley of Death	Psalm 23	the psalmist
Valley of Dry Bones	Ezekiel 37	Israel

Antagonist	Giants	Meaning
Canaanites	giants (the Anakim) living in the Promised Land	a valley where you can choose to trust
Canaanites	a giant-sized army: nine hundred iron chariots among King Jabin's forces	a valley where you can choose to face your battles with courage and conviction
Philistines	Goliath, a Philistine giant	a valley where you can choose to stay brave when the odds are against you
unsafe people and the depths of hardship	the giants of threat and danger	a valley where you can choose to follow the Good Shepherd through many dangers
Babylonian exile	the giants of hopelessness and death	a valley where you can choose to let God resurrect your hope

Each **Storyline Bible Study** is five lessons long and can be paired with its thematic partner for a seamless, ten-week study. Complement the *Valleys* study with

MOUNTAINS
REDISCOVERING YOUR VISION AND
RESTORING YOUR HOPE IN GOD'S PRESENCE

In the ancient, symbol-driven world of the Bible, location didn't just matter—it had meaning. The *Mountains* Bible study will guide you through five mountaintop Bible stories because mountains are holy ground for connecting with God.

LESSON ONE: Becoming Secure in Your Identity
Mount of Creation: Where God Launches the World
GENESIS 1–2

LESSON TWO: Believing God Loves You No Matter What
Mount Sinai: Where God Gives the Israelites the Mosaic Law
EXODUS 19–20

LESSON THREE: Reconstructing Your Faith in an Age of Deconstruction
Mount of the Sermon: Where Jesus Delivers
His Most Famous Message
MATTHEW 5

LESSON FOUR: Growing Hopeful When Your Life Is Hard
Mount of Transfiguration: Where Jesus Reveals His Glory
to Peter, James, and John
MATTHEW 17

LESSON FIVE: Relying on God's Presence to Carry You Through
Mount of the Great Commission: Where Jesus
Commissions His Disciples
MATTHEW 28

Learn more at thestorylineproject.com.

CP1820

Storyline Bible Studies

Each study follows people, places, or things throughout the Bible. This approach allows you to see the cohesive storyline of Scripture and appreciate the Bible as the literary masterpiece that it is.

Access free resources to help you teach or lead a small group at thestorylineproject.com.

Coming Soon: *Sinners* and *Saints*

 STORYLINE

CP1816

Acknowledgments

WITHOUT MY FAMILY'S SUPPORT, the **Storyline Bible Studies** would just be a dream. I'm exceedingly grateful for a family that prays and cheers for me when I step out to try something new. To my husband, Aaron, son, Caleb, and mom, Noemi: You three sacrificed the most to ensure that I had enough time and space to write. Thank you. And to all my extended family: I know an army of Armstrongs was praying and my family in Austin was cheering me on to the finish line. Thank you.

To my ministry partners at the Polished Network, Integrus Leadership, and Dallas Bible Church: Linking arms with you made this project possible. I love doing Kingdom work with you.

NavPress and Tyndale teams: Thank you for believing in me. You wholeheartedly embraced the concept, and you've made this project better in every way possible. Special thanks to David Zimmerman, my amazing editor Caitlyn Carlson, Elizabeth Schroll, Olivia Eldredge, David Geeslin, and the entire editorial and marketing teams.

Teresa Swanstrom Anderson: Thank you for connecting me with Caitlyn. You'll forever go down in history as the person who made my dreams come true.

Jana Burson: You were the catalyst. Thank you for being my agent.

Lastly, I want to thank my early readers: Warren Truesdale, Sharifa Stevens, Jason and Tiffany Stein, and Jayme Hightower. Your feedback was invaluable. Thank you for believing in me and devoting so much of your time to the early manuscripts.

Resources for Deeper Study

OLD TESTAMENT

Bearing God's Name: Why Sinai Still Matters by Carmen Joy Imes

By the River Chebar: Historical, Literary, and Theological Studies in the Book of Ezekiel by Daniel I. Block

The Epic of Eden: A Christian Entry into the Old Testament by Sandra L. Richter

NEW TESTAMENT

Echoes of Scripture in the Gospels by Richard B. Hays

The Gospels as Stories: A Narrative Approach to Matthew, Mark, Luke, and John by Jeannine K. Brown

BIBLE STUDY

Commentary on the New Testament Use of the Old Testament, eds. G. K. Beale and D. A. Carson

Dictionary of Biblical Imagery, eds. Leland Ryken, James C. Wilhoit, and Tremper Longman III

The Drama of Scripture: Finding Our Place in the Biblical Story by Craig G. Bartholomew and Michael W. Goheen

How (Not) to Read the Bible: Making Sense of the Anti-Women, Anti-Science, Pro-Violence, Pro-Slavery and Other Crazy Sounding Parts of Scripture by Dan Kimball

How to Read the Bible as Literature . . . and Get More Out of It by Leland Ryken

Literarily: How Understanding Bible Genres Transforms Bible Study by Kristie Anyabwile

The Mission of God: Unlocking the Bible's Grand Narrative by Christopher J. H. Wright

"Reading Scripture as a Coherent Story" by Richard Bauckham, in *The Art of Reading Scripture*, eds. Ellen F. Davis and Richard B. Hays

Reading While Black: African American Biblical Interpretation as an Exercise in Hope by Esau McCaulley

Read the Bible for a Change: Understanding and Responding to God's Word by Ray Lubeck

Scripture as Communication: Introducing Biblical Hermeneutics by Jeannine K. Brown

What Is the Bible and How Do We Understand It? by Dennis R. Edwards

Words of Delight: A Literary Introduction to the Bible by Leland Ryken

About the Author

KAT ARMSTRONG was born in Houston, Texas, where the humidity ruins her Mexi-German curls. She is a powerful voice in our generation as a sought-after Bible teacher, preacher, coach, and innovative ministry leader. She holds a master's degree from Dallas Theological Seminary and is the author of *No More Holding Back*, *The In-Between Place*, and the **Storyline Bible Studies**. In 2008, Kat cofounded the Polished Network to embolden working women in their faith and work. As the host of *The Polished Podcast* and *The Emboldened Woman Podcast*, she interviews working women at the crossroads of faith and work and offers devotionals from the Scriptures. Kat is the director of leadership processes for Integrus Leadership and is pursuing a doctorate of ministry in New Testament context at Northern Seminary. She and her husband, Aaron, have been married for nineteen years; live in Dallas, Texas, with their son, Caleb; and attend Dallas Bible Church, where Aaron serves as the lead pastor.

KATARMSTRONG.COM
@KATARMSTRONG1

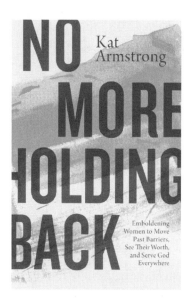

Make peace with your past.

Find hope in the present.

Step into your future.

Notes

LESSON ONE | TRUSTING GOD WITH YOUR GIANT-SIZED DOUBTS

1. Credit for this phrase goes to DeWayne Blackwell and Earl "Bud" Lee, writers of a song made famous by Garth Brooks: "Friends in Low Places," *No Fences* © 1990 Capitol Nashville.
2. See, for example, Blue Letter Bible, "Lexicon: Strong's H812— *'eškōl*," accessed March 31, 2022, www.blueletterbible.org/lexicon/h812/niv/wlc/0-1.
3. John H. Sailhamer, *The Pentateuch as Narrative: A Biblical-Theological Commentary* (Grand Rapids, MI: Zondervan, 1992), 388.

LESSON TWO | FACING YOUR BATTLES WITH COURAGE AND CONVICTION

1. Ron Pierce, "Deborah: Only When a Good Man Is Hard to Find?" in *Vindicating the Vixens: Revisiting Sexualized, Vilified, and Marginalized Women of the Bible*, ed. Sandra Glahn (Grand Rapids, MI: Kregel, 2017), 194.
2. Richard Bauckham, *Gospel Women: Studies of the Named Women in the Gospels* (Grand Rapids, MI: Eerdmans, 2002), 275.
3. Pierce, "Deborah," 198.
4. As quoted in Richard D. Patterson, "The View from the Valley," Bible.org, October 30, 2010, https://bible.org/article/view-valley#P33_9362.

LESSON THREE | STAYING BRAVE WHEN THE ODDS ARE AGAINST YOU

1. "Harriet Tubman," Africans in America, pbs.org, accessed March 9, 2022, https://www.pbs.org/wgbh/aia/part4/4p1535.html.

2. "Harriet Tubman," ed. Debra Michals, National Women's History Museum, 2015, https://www.womenshistory.org/education-resources/biographies/harriet-tubman.

3. "Harriet Tubman: The 'Moses' of Her People," *Christianity Today*, August 8, 2008, https://www.christianitytoday.com/history/people/activists/harriet-tubman.html.

LESSON FOUR | RESISTING FEAR WHEN YOUR LIFE BOTTOMS OUT

1. Eugene H. Peterson, *As Kingfishers Catch Fire: A Conversation on the Ways of God Formed by the Words of God* (Colorado Springs: Waterbrook, 2017), 103.

2. This chart is from Brueggemann and Bellinger, *Psalms*, 2. Reproduced with permission of Cambridge University Press through PLSclear.

3. Ellen T. Charry, *Psalms 1–50: Brazos Theological Commentary on the Bible* (Grand Rapids, MI: Brazos Press, 2015), 116.

4. W. H. Bellinger Jr., *Psalms: A Guide to Studying the Psalter*, second ed. (Grand Rapids, MI: Baker Academic, 2012), 106.

5. Tremper Longman III, *How to Read the Psalms* (Downers Grove, IL: InterVarsity Press, 1988), 31.

6. Ben Witherington III, *Psalms Old and New: Exegesis, Intertextuality, and Hermeneutics* (Minneapolis: Fortress Press, 2017), xv.

7. Walter Brueggemann and William H. Bellinger Jr., *Psalms: New Cambridge Bible Commentary* (New York: Cambridge University Press, 2014), 23.

8. William P. Brown, "Psalms," in *Theological Bible Commentary*, ed. Gail R. O'Day and David L. Petersen (Louisville: Westminister John Knox Press, 2009), 177.

9. Witherington, *Psalms Old and New*, 4.

10. Charry, *Psalms 1–50*, 117.

11. Peterson, *Kingfishers*, 101.

12. Rolf A. Jacobson, "Psalm 23: You Are with Me," in Nancy deClaissé-Walford, Rolf A. Jacobson, and Beth LaNeel Tanner, *The Book of Psalms: The New International Commentary on the Old Testament* (Grand Rapids, MI: Eerdmans, 2014), 241.

13. Robert Alter, *The Book of Psalms: A Translation with Commentary* (New York: W. W. Norton, 2007), 78.

14. Jacobson, "Psalm 23," in *The Book of Psalms*, 243.

15. Federico Villanueva, *Psalms 1–72: A Pastoral and Contextual Commentary*, Asia Bible Commentary (Carlisle, Cumbria, UK: Langham, 2016), 141.

16. Peterson, *Kingfishers*, 103.

17. Brueggemann and Bellinger, *Psalms*, 125.

18. Peterson, *Kingfishers*, 102.

19. Peterson, *Kingfishers*, 105.

20. Jacobson, "Psalm 23," in *The Book of Psalms*, 239.

LESSON FIVE | RESURRECTING HOPE WHEN YOUR CONFIDENCE IN GOD IS LOST

1. "Osteoporosis," Mayo Clinic, August 21, 2021, https://www.mayoclinic.org/diseases-conditions/osteoporosis/symptoms-causes/syc-20351968.

2. Whitney Woollard, "Ezekiel's Bizarre Calling: This Book Can Be Difficult to Digest," BibleProject, accessed March 9, 2022, https://bibleproject.com/blog/ezekiels-bizarre-calling.

3. Daniel I. Block, *By the River Chebar: Historical, Literary, and Theological Studies in the Book of Ezekiel* (Eugene, OR: Cascade Books, 2013), 27.

4. Block, *By the River Chebar*, xi.

5. Dexter E. Callender Jr., "Exodus," in *The Africana Bible: Reading Israel's Scriptures from Africa and the African Diaspora*, ed. Hugh R. Page Jr. (Minneapolis: Fortress Press, 2010), 161.

6. Fleming Rutledge, "Nothing More True," in *And God Spoke to Abraham: Preaching from the Old Testament* (Grand Rapids, MI: Eerdmans, 2011), 347.

7. Brian Neil Peterson, *Ezekiel in Context: Ezekiel's Message Understood in Its Historical Setting of Covenant Curses and Ancient Near Eastern Mythological Motifs* (Eugene, OR: Pickwick Publications, 2012), 233.

8. Peterson, *Ezekiel in Context*, 233–234, 290.

9. Eliya Mohol, "Ezekiel," in *South Asia Bible Commentary: A One-Volume Commentary on the Whole Bible*, ed. Brian Wintle (Grand Rapids, MI: Zondervan, 2015), 1073.

10. Mark Driscoll, *The Rise and Fall of Mars Hill*, produced by Mike Cosper, *Christianity Today*, https://www.christianitytoday.com/ct/podcasts/rise-and-fall-of-mars-hill.